Babyloving
The Emotional Life of a Baby

Hiag Akmakjian

riverrun

Copyright © 2015 Hiag Akmakjian

Published by riverrun publishing, LLC 2015

www.riverrunpublishing.com

All rights reserved

No part of this book may be reproduced in any form or by any electronic or mechanical means including information storage and retrieval systems, without permission in writing from the author. The only exception is by a reviewer, who may quote short excerpts in a review

ISBN- 978-0-9888367-6-1

*for Margaret –
with love*

Why do roses appear in the spring, grain in the summer, and grapes in the fall? Things need time to grow, to develop what is in them. Otherwise tiny children would turn suddenly into fully grown adults, and trees would shoot up out of the earth. But these do not happen. Everything grows gradually, which is natural, and they grow from a specific seed and each retains its specific character. We could say that each grows and is nourished by its innate substance.

Lucretius, *On the Nature of Things*

WE BEGIN LIFE in another's arms, and how those arms hold and snuggle us begins to shape our feelings about ourselves and others – about the world and life itself.

In the creation of a human being, uterine life is only the first of two gestations. The uterus does its job to perfection. It assembles a new human organism from an assortment of chemical compounds. Then, at birth, a second, more critical gestation begins: psychological gestation.

Psychological gestation is a much more complex development. And it lasts longer. It goes on for thirty-six months, four times as long as life in the uterus.

Only on the completion of psychological gestation does the baby become an autonomous human being. That is, the baby becomes not just physically independent but – immensely important – psychologically independent as well.

As the baby grows into a little child, he or she attains a separate identity – a sense of self.

Maybe we tend not to think of psychological development as "gestation part two" because it doesn't take place inside the uterus but outside, in the world, where we can see it happening. Or maybe because it doesn't happen as smoothly and automatically as it did in the uterus, where almost no matter what the mother and father did in their daily living, the baby's physiology proceeded without effort: the fœtus's heart continued to beat, cells reproduced, glands developed.

But psychological development is different. The psyche is sensitive and susceptible to all manner of influence. Psychological gestation goes on happening everywhere, all the time – playing in the kitchen or in the schoolyard, sitting on Daddy's lap, lolling on the floor, splashing mud puddles with the little girl next door. While all these events are happening, a new and enlarging experience of the world is taken into the psyche.

When this second gestation ends, around the age of three or four, the baby attains "psychological birth." It's called psychological birth because only then is the toddler emotionally ready to continue through childhood and adolescence and become fully an adult.

During this long second gestation, the baby begins to form ties. The infant who in the beginning is a bundle of reflexes and sensations, and needs and demands, grows into a toddler and begins to be a person who relates to others – an interacting being. The baby becomes capable of moods and emotions. During these first three years – to look ahead a bit – the baby, and child, will develop into a feeling being, with emotions ranging from anger and rage to affection and possessiveness, from hate and envy to love and jealousy. A newborn baby has none of these emotions.

Physiologically, you can get some idea of the rapid advances of the infant by considering that the baby not so long ago was a single cell. The cell divided into two, and the two became four. That first feat, of one cell becoming two, took a whole day, twenty-four hours, to achieve. But now, the newborn in the mother's arms creates out of her milk uncountable thousands of cells a minute—ten thousand a day of brain cells alone. Between birth and the time when the first teeth begin to come in at five or six months, the brain doubles in weight and the nervous system grows hugely more complex.

The microscopic structure of the nervous system resembles a wood in winter full of bare trees. From each trunk, lacy branches of neurons reach toward surrounding branches, tip ends intermingling and almost but not quite touching. As the filigree structure grows in more thickly and the wood becomes a dense forest, the brain goes from a biological entity, a cell mass, to a functioning organ, a mind. The cells, at the outset mere physical matter mechanically dividing, cross the ever-mysterious line between matter and mind and become the consciousness of a person, one who in time might solve problems in topological transformation series or translate Andrew Marvell from English into Swahili.

During infancy, most of the baby's processing of information and memory storage takes place in the mid-brain. One of the brain's major tasks during the first year of life is to have the cells branch out and connect to as many other cells as possible, and also to become myelinated: sheathed with a protein cover that dramatically speeds up the transmission of information.

When the baby's brain is physically fully developed, sometime late in the first year, it will have grown to a hundred billion neurons. Each individual neuron will be capable of making hundreds of thousands of connections with each of the other cells of the brain and nervous system in an extraordinarily intricate crisscross of wiring, ready to surge into operation with a passing thought.

At the very beginning, babies are all need. They need to be kept warm and dry, they need to be fed, they need to be cradled in arms, they need to be softly spoken to. They need to be understood and soothed. At times, babies' needs can be very taxing to parents or care givers. Fortunately most parents usually feel a ready willingness to make allowances, even when demands sometimes are great.

They do it because they sense that adult rules of behavior don't apply. When a baby cries from hunger, or wants to be held and gently rocked, they know the baby is not ordering them around. There are of course some parents who still believe those old folk tales. But babies not having our intelligence can't think the way we do. They don't know enough about people and behavior to manipulate or give orders. As long ago as the eighteenth-century, the French philosopher Jean-Jacques Rousseau wrote: "Childhood has its own way of seeing, thinking, and feeling, and nothing is more foolish than to try to substitute ours for theirs." (An example of early "logic": a boy of four told his mother he didn't want to go out at night "because I'll get the dark all over me.")

Child developmentalists take a view similar to Rousseau's: "Children . . . are not adults in miniature. They are beings per se, different from their elders in their mental nature, their functioning, their understanding of events, and their reactions to them."*

Babies don't really have a mind yet, a brain capable of thou<u>ght. They have only a "body-mind</u>". They emerge from the uterus fully equipped with fingers, toes, a pair of eyes and

---

* See 'Notes' for all references and quoted material

a tongue as delicate as a bird's. But the brain, the apparatus for understanding, is still largely unformed and will not be fully formed until about nine months after birth. The brain and nervous system are a sensing mechanism to keep the organism stable. The psyche acts mostly in reflex.

It's obvious, then, that newborns can't start with ideas of relatedness—like "mother and baby", for example. That is sophisticated knowledge. They don't know yet that they're separate beings, that there's something called a "mother" and something else called a "baby" and that they are the latter only. They "think" (which is to say, they feel and sense with all their being) that whatever they see and hear and taste is a part of themselves. There is no idea yet of what's outside their body or what's inside. In fact there is no self yet for things to be inside or outside of. There are not even things yet. Babies don't differentiate: baby and mother are a single being, and everything they experience of the outside world is part of this being.

Gradually, however, the newborn begins to notice differences in faces. But in this initial stage, all faces are interchangeable. Anybody could be "Mother" (the mothering person), even care givers. Grandma or father could be "Mother", and we know from reports that even wolves in the wild have been known to "mother" human babies. The ethologist Konrad Lorenz, studying ducks, discovered that when he squatted and quacked and waddled across the barnyard, newborn ducks happily lined up and waddled behind him, believing that this enormous squatting "duck" was their mother. On hatching, they had imprinted on him. It is in this same sense that there is no "Mother" or "Father" to a newborn infant. The baby could "imprint" on anyone. Happily, we are wired to imprint by preference on humans.

There is, though, an unconscious expectation –of some vague unnamable something. That's all that the term mother can mean at the beginning: an expectation.

The expectation is of nurture. That is why a baby's "mother" could be father, mother, granny or anyone. But we'll see that for good and compelling reasons, it should, however, consistently be the same mothering person—a topic we will return to again. To the newborn, "mothering" is not just being fed or kept dry and warm. Even more important, "mothering" is a loving care, a comforting touch—it is being stroked and rocked in "maternal" arms.

PLEASURE AND UNPLEASURE

Psychologists believe that as faces come in and out of the newborn's ken, they are like hallucinations. Does the baby actually see the parent's face? Or is the face only something that the baby is imagining? Probably it is a little of both to a baby—at least, as far as anyone knows.

When the face drifts away, or whatever it is that faces do when they're no longer there, it's as though the baby has stopped imagining it. That may sound farfetched to us but to a baby it would make the purest sense. It's literally a case of out of sight, out of mind. After all, the sensation of hunger causes the baby to squirm, fidget and cry and then suddenly the face appears. Therefore, it's "obviously" the baby's squirming, fidgeting and crying that "created" the face. Since both experiences happen together, to a baby it seems perfectly reasonable to understand it as cause and effect. At this age, correlation is proof.

On occasion, when the face is up close, something touches a certain part of the baby's skin—the lips and the mouth—in a way that sends an exciting signal: sucking exertions follow, and the baby begins to feel a suffuse liquid warmth. A sensual pleasure builds.

Pleasure always follows the sucking and warm liquidness: hunger subsides, contentment returns. After this has occurred once, twice, many times, a rhythm establishes itself: the pleasure is followed by a slow return of discomfort, which is again followed by pleasure.

But if the discomfort is allowed to go on for too long and becomes pain, the familiar pleasure does not return, and hunger turns into something disquieting. Hunger can even be feared if the discomfort is prolonged and turns into something painful. The sensation is intolerable. Adults in psychoanalysis suffering from depression, bulimia or anorexia, or other disorders involving drugs or alcohol, can often trace their difficulties to their earliest infancy.

Despite some claims that scheduled feeding—feeding according to the clock and not hunger—is passé, it is still practiced in quite a number of homes despite its harmful effect. And understaffed daycare facilities pretty much have no choice in the matter. But scheduled feeding is too important to be gone over rapidly – there will be more to say.

But in the best circumstances, the baby's experience is, most of the time, one of contentment or pleasure, or at least the absence of prolonged discomfort. And in this initial period, of oral appetites and gratifications, as long as contented feelings predominate over distress, the quiet wellbeing of uterine life continues unaffected. Tensions are kept to a minimum and a calm serenity establishes itself inside the baby—quite the best atmosphere for promoting development.

During the first weeks, the baby experiences everything in a highly simple, global way: the world is a profusion of haphazard sensations: splotches of color, pleasant tastes, intriguing smells, changes in temperature, sounds and noises followed by the serenity of silence. All of these experiences register on the psyche and the baby tries to make sense of them.

To the newborn, the world is a strangeness that only very gradually becomes unstrange.

William James, the great psychologist, imagined that life to a newborn is "one great blooming, buzzing confusion." He thought it was too much to say even that an infant has "the consciousness of something there, a mere this . . . [because] even the term this would perhaps be too discriminative." He believed that only one word might express the newborn's experience of life, "the bare interjection 'lo!'"

To begin with, the baby's world is "objectless". That is, the newborn does not yet distinguish between physical objects. And—in the other sense, the "self and object" sense, meaning the self and the other person—the baby can't tell clearly the difference between people or even the difference between them and the baby's own self (which is still only forming).

The baby lives in a vague Whatever. There are no boundaries to this Whatever. It is all baby. The sensation of a nipple in the newborn's mouth means that the nipple is part of the baby. At this stage, we can speculate that the baby feels something like omnipotence.

For the newborn, suckling, urinating, defecating, coughing, sneezing, squirming – all have the same effect: they discharge tension. In infancy especially, we seem to want to maintain the unstressed, stable experience of uterine existence. If the newborn's experience of life can be likened to anything, it is to the mystic's goal of perfect dreamlike oneness with the universe, a sense of unboundedness and blissful union. Babies don't have to attain a sense of union. They are born with it. (It's ironic that what adults describe as the "ultimate" experience in life is actually life's first.) As so many myths inform us, we start out in this Eden and then leave it behind forever. Though we sometimes feel a nostalgia for a legend we call "the past"—"legend" because the past can never be more than a blur of reality and imagination—the compensations of advancing development are too pleasurable for any serious regret over the loss.

THE BABY'S ENLARGING EXPERIENCE

At first, then, there is no one but the baby, but this begins to change when the baby learns that sometimes crying does not make the face appear. And when the face does not appear, the discomfort of hunger pains doesn't subside but grows more intense. Crying and fussing, apparently, are not what bring relief, at least not by themselves. Something else must happen. The baby doesn't know yet what.

As the baby grows during the days and weeks that follow, frustration and gratification slowly establish a rhythm. The regularity has a reassuring quality. It indicates that gratification can be relied on. There may be frustrations, but gratification has always been there when needed and will soon follow again, and all will be well, just as before.

When needs are consistently satisfied, a degree of frustration begins to be bearable. The baby perceives that frustration is not a permanent pain, and knowing that makes it easier to bear. A tolerance begins to build.

FRUSTRATION TOLERANCE

The baby acquires frustration tolerance as we all did—at a snail's pace. It has taken years for us to know what we know about living and to be able to handle setbacks. Part of a parent's job is to be a regulator, making certain that the dosage of frustration fits the baby's abilities. Acting as the baby's guardian, good-enough parents take great care to gauge the amount of tolerance that would be comfortable, and only as they feel it's right do they step things up a notch—and never at the very beginning of life. They don't need to induce frustration deliberately: small daily frustrations are never lacking.

Parents sense that the way to build tolerance is by supplying an occasional generous dollop of gratification. That acts as a counterbalance. They might, for example, pick up and snuggle the baby even though the baby might not need to be hugged at that moment. The gratification both protects and encourages the baby. It builds a store of good feelings. These steady supplies of pleasure feel to the baby like expressions of love, and it is the baby's pleasure at feeling loved that makes the discomfort of frustrations endurable.

(At a later stage of development, it would be a mistake to bend over backward and eliminate every bit of frustration: an artificially protected childhood is a poor preparation for reality. The more you attempt to create a life of no frustration, the more easily will the child be knocked down by even small frustrations. But remember that that comes later. In the early months, the baby needs as much pleasure and contentment as possible. The baby in fact needs coddling at this age, the better to face life's inevitable frustrations later.)

THE VALUE OF FRUSTRATION—IN VERY SMALL DOSES

As large amounts of pleasure make it possible for frustrations to be absorbed in increasing numbers, frustrations soon begin to be seen as what they are: moments to be passed through, not the end of the world. In the opposite kind of case—where there have been too many frustrations too soon—frustration tolerance has no opportunity to build, and then even slight discomforts seem too difficult to contend with. That sabotages something important: the creative role of frustration.

It may sound strange to speak of frustration as having a creative side. But after the first six months, frustration in small doses promotes the stretching of frustration tolerance. That in turn increases the ability to confront reality. A need doesn't have to be met the very moment it makes itself felt. Pleasures don't have to arrive immediately for the baby to know they will be reliably supplied. By that age, the baby knows better and is confident, grows patient. The mother signals the end of a frustration by her appearance—or voice—which helps the baby to believe that relief is coming and be able to tolerate the frustration a minute or two longer.

FRUSTRATION AND DIFFERENTIATION

But just as important, frustration serves another purpose. It contributes to differentiating the self from others. A frustration emphasizes that the baby has limits: if everything were "me," there would be no frustration. How would the "me" frustrate the "me"? Therefore there must be a "me" and a "not me." In this small way, stirrings of a sense of self move a step ahead with each (tolerable) dose of frustration.

Since frustration has benefits, why wouldn't it make sense to start frustrating early? Because too much frustration overwhelms—it traumatizes. Then nothing is learned. Trauma means injury, pain, shock, and you don't "adjust" to shock. Only panic results. Progress is impaired as impatience takes root (think of the driver at the traffic light who shouts "Come on, come on!" to make the light turn green). Prolonged frustration creates hopelessness. Depressives often express hopelessness ("What's the use? Why bother?") and see no possibility of relief from their suffering and give up trying.

MAKING TRUST AND CHOICE POSSIBLE

That's why demand feeding is so important. Child developmentalists make a point of urging that the baby not be fed according to the clock or some convenient schedule. Demand feeding satisfies not just the stomach but emotional needs also.

Scheduled feeding does just the reverse: it starves emotional needs, and frustrates the baby—severely so. That could only lead to problems later in life.

People who are afraid of "spoiling" their child sometimes deprive their baby of a feeding and harden themselves to the baby's crying. They feel that if they give in to the first few demands, the baby will learn to keep demanding. That leaves the baby in a helpless, expectant state. Taught by misguided "experts" to think in a certain way, these parents don't see that if the baby is crying out of hunger, deprivation is cruelty.

It can't be stressed enough that crying is a signal that something is wrong. Its purpose—in all young creatures—is to get immediate help in whatever form is needed. Human babies no more cry to "manipulate" their parents than kittens, puppies, calves or colts make their distress calls to manipulate their mothers.

Frustration tolerance contributes to another important development. It fosters the child's ability to be patient and wait. It creates a confident anticipation of results. Patience in turn makes it possible—allows time—to weigh pros and cons. And it is only when you can weigh both the pros and cons of something that you can exercise choice.

The capacity to wait enables the infant to exert control over urges and postpone (a little while) the satisfaction of needs. Feeling unpressured, the baby becomes more alert to surroundings, confident that things will go smoothly. A small amount of trust has already started to build, beautiful to behold (and never to be squashed!).

COMPULSIVITY AND THE "HURRIED CHILD"

When frustrations outpace gratification, compulsive behavior creeps in. No matter how small a pleasure might be, at least it's a pleasure, and if pleasures are few and far between, each must be seized on. There must be no delay between need and satisfaction.

This predisposes the baby to being a "hurried child," impatient. When a feeding does arrive, it is emotionally lunged at—as though the baby were thinking, "Grab it while the grabbing's good." There is a temptation to stay with what at least seems pleasurable and avoid painful reality. (It is only a step from this to the addictions of adolescence and adulthood, those notorious avoidances of reality: addictions not just to drugs and alcohol but to food and love and sex and romance novels and shopping and TV and even theft—a long list.)

There is no adulthood separate from infancy. Trust and choice and the ability to wait become a fundamental part of the person and have a far-reaching effect on adult functioning.

Look at it in reverse. The infant who has been deprived of timely gratification and who has consequently never learned to tolerate any delay in pleasure becomes the adult forever driven by the infantile mode of functioning: with impatience and anxiety, with panic. Without regard for consequences (infants are not capable of viewing things that way), their behavior has one aim only: like the newborn's, to discharge tension at once. That a given pleasure might bring harm in its wake is not considered—even though it is known. Adult alcoholics, for example, continue to drink even knowing its harmfulness and the damage they are causing themselves.

A baby who has been given appropriate gratification and can tolerate some delay in pleasure grows up to be a person able to postpone pleasure for a moment and tolerate small discomforts. This moment of discomfort gives time to reflect on alternatives, time to consider consequences and choose according to long-range advantage. The baby, more able to resist the pressures of instinctual demands, develops sounder thinking and judgment. Where you have that, thought and judgment, being unrushed, are no longer the prey of every impulse, leading sometimes to self-defeating acts.

THE GOOD KIND OF AGGRESSION: AS USABLE ENERGY

We are all born with a certain amount of psychic energy, and some of it has an aggressive character. (Without "aggressive energy" it would not be possible to get out of a chair and cross a room.) But it's as though the psyche has only a certain amount of it. Whatever portion of aggressive energy remains in its original state, raw and "untamed," leaves that much less available for development to use. And that means that development suffers.

If we think of aggressivity in this benign sense, our development is powered by it – and also by love. (If the word "aggressive" sounds too hostile, think of it as "assertiveness".) A blend of love and this benign aggressiveness, or assertiveness, powers all our actions and thoughts. It powers our life. The blending of love and aggressiveness helps us accomplish whatever we set out to do. Without the taming, aggressive energy remains in its raw form. It remains aggressive in the "bad" sense of the word.

It's like racing a car's engine. If you step on the accelerator, the engine will roar with impressive power and use up all your fuel, but the car won't move. To get the car to go, you must first put the engine in gear. With the energy thus "tamed," the car can go.

This converting of raw aggressivity to usable energy is fundamentally important to the whole of development—for the rest of the person's life:

A baby's emotional development is best helped when this taming happens during the first five months. If not, all the rest of development – throughout life – will not derive maximum benefits.

The idea is an important one to understand and it is worth stressing. Love does the taming. And in the beginning, "love" is simply meeting the baby's needs. The need might be hunger. Or it might be asking to be cuddled. When the baby's needs are abundantly met, this comes across as "love" and it fuses with aggressive energy. That's the "taming": the fusing together of love and aggressiveness. It is a psychological energy. What would otherwise be a futile gunning of the engine and using up of fuel becomes psychological energy available for development.

THE DOUBLE FEEDING: THE BREAST AND THE MOTHER'S SMILES

The story of emotional development is the story of becoming an individual. But it is also the story of becoming a self relating to others.

It has begun to dawn on the fledgling awareness that no matter how strenuous the baby's attempts at getting rid of discomforts, they simply do not get wished away. The technique obstinately fails—though that does not convince the baby to abandon faith in it, not for many years. Power, even the illusion of power, is never given up easily.

Discomfort seems to stop only with the return of the face. First the face appears. Then there comes a pleasantly woozy sensation of being lifted, and then getting warmly snuggled against a yielding, sweet-smelling softness from which a voluptuous liquidity flows. Gradually the discomfort relents and pleasure returns. This, the fundamental experience of the first weeks of life, becomes the baby's first human relation.

Among the baby's perceptions, the face plays an important part: that's what the baby looks at, not the breast. The face is at just the right distance for the feeding baby's eyes to focus on comfortably: around 35 centimeters, or 14 inches. The mother (or mothering person) smiles at the baby, and the baby takes in the smile along with the milk in a double "feeding."

The baby seems not to feel any particular emotion in this experience beyond perhaps a sense that things are as they should be. But during the many hours of successive feedings, the baby has much time to reflect on the smiling face, on the sensation of being held, on the soft feel of the breast, on the warm liquidity in the mouth. The baby gradually understands that these components of the feeling of wellbeing all go together with the face. At this stage, the baby can take in "mother" (the consistent nurturer) only when the person is present. It will not be until the fourth year that "object constancy" will develop fully. Object constancy is the understanding and feeling that the mother exists even when she is not there.

It is easy to imagine how the baby might develop a hazy notion that the mother's face is part of the baby. If the baby has a need, the face magically appears—and then no more need.

FROM PASSIVE MODE TO ACTIVE

Fresh impressions keep coming in and piling up. By around the middle of the second month, the baby becomes aware that certain impressions seem to match others. But the prime candidate is the mother's face: the baby has lately begun to be aware that it is not a different face each time but the same face every time. This is an indicator of an important new development:

Memory proper has begun—memory as something more than repeat impressions. The impressions are linked together and held in storage.

With memory, development steps up its pace. It is memory that connects the baby's sensation of hunger with the expectation that gratification will come. If gratification was available a while ago, it will be available again. The baby fusses, the mother responds, the need is met.

How neat. The idea that things are associated takes root: a signal is learned. It goes like this. Fussing communicates need. The communication is understood. The need is responded to.

We might note in this something else too, an invaluable bit of new knowledge: the baby learns that effort brings results. The feeling "I have influence over events" can start as early as at three to six months. By the same token, it can be hampered at that early age too.

True, this chain of effort and power plays into the baby's delusion of omnipotence, which, though losing its force, continues to resist surrender (as it temporarily should). It will for quite some time. For now the feeling of omnipotence is important for development: it helps build feelings of mastery. "I—[this "I" is mostly still a bundle of sensations]—I have executive ability and by my strivings I can effect change. I fuss, I stir—and things get done."

With changes like these, the baby slowly becomes capable of more focused behavior. No longer the totally helpless birthling, or even the relatively more sophisticated one- or two-month-old, the several-month-old baby is in the position now of "doing" something about needs rather than feeling at the mercy of the Whatever.

HOLDING AND TOUCHING

What makes possible this subtle shift from passive to active is the feeling that the baby is cared for. The mother's lovingly holding the baby instills the sense of all's well. Holding, which began in the uterus, has broadened to include "touch" experiences: handling, hugging, feeding.

The experience of "being held" gets internalized. That is, the baby takes it in, makes it part of the psyche. That's why babies don't feel abandoned when they are put down in their crib. For a little while, the lingering memory of being held continues to provide comfort. Somewhere inside them, they feel held.

Donald W. Winnicott, a renowned British pediatrician-psychoanalyst, created the phrase "the holding experience" and assigned great importance to it. He said in-arms holding gives the baby the sense that the environment (at first that means only the mother and the father) is reliable. He spoke of the holding experience's symbolic extension beyond infancy and throughout development: the family "holds" the individual and society "holds" the family. Winnicott meant "holding" in a healthy sense. When things go wrong developmentally, the growing child and later the adult seek all sorts of unhealthy ways to find the holding that was not there when it was needed, and some, as we shall see, turn to drugs and other stimulants.

CARRYING ("GESTATION") AND HOLDING

Intrauterine carrying terminates at birth. The external carrying, the in-arms experience, begins at birth and in a sense never stops.

For the human infant, being born not just dependent but precariously dependent, the in-arms holding is as vital to health and wellbeing as feeding. When at ease with life, the baby relaxes. The delicate body molds itself against the mother's chest and stomach, and the pressure of the warm contact makes the baby's skin and muscles feel "right."

The molding is reassuring as the contours of the baby's body melt into the mother's torso. Her heartbeat, smell, sounds and movements seem like the baby's own. We recall that to a baby at the youngest age, boundaries between mother and infant are nonexistent. Mother and baby are a not-yet-differentiated being.

The mother too, if she enjoys having the baby, feels a profound contentment at the molding. She savors the baby's instinctively curling against her in a peaceful fusing of bodies and feels an accompanying pleasant languor. The even tenor of the uterine experience, that extraordinary journey from single cell to complex fetus, in being thus extended, bolsters the baby's delusion of continued union.

And with that, by the way, goes the important sense that life is good.

THE SENSE OF TOUCH AND SECURITY

Skin contact, the being touched by another is, according to the anthropologist and author Ashley Montagu, an under-appreciated pleasure. In his classic book *Touching*, he eloquently explains the intimate connection between human ties and touching, and love and sensuality.

Touching is the most durable of the five senses. It comes to life in the embryo at least as early as the eighth week after conception, long before the other four senses, and continues until death. Even if a person goes blind and deaf, even after taste and smell have failed, the sense of touch remains.

The senses make up only a part of the baby's experience. Another part is the feelings, and the two work hand in hand. We said that the first "sense" of life is of a strangeness, which is felt to be vaguely dangerous, the way many new and unexpected sensations feel. But the sensation of being held is different. Its charge of emotional satisfaction creates a feeling of security.

One of the best parental helps to development is to pick the baby up—gently, not impatiently, not with a scowl, not dutifully or "because it's good for development." Most mothers hold the baby in their arms rather than a plastic bassinet, sensing that babies need to feel warm skin against warm skin. And mother and baby can see each other's face.

Bassinets force the baby to face away from the mother, and there's something emotionally cold about that. It doesn't give as much of the "all's well" feeling that the baby gets from being snuggled against the mother's chest or shoulder. The people who invented those cloth devices that snuggle even the tiniest infant against Mum or Dad for hours at a time deserve the thanks of a generation.

Louise J. Kaplan, in Oneness and Separateness: From Infant to Individual says that each time the baby is allowed to take the breast in a way that makes good use of his inborn knowledge of head-turning, holding on and sucking, the baby has an experience of harmony and well-being. Being understood in this way is what we mean by "being held."

When caregivers respond to the baby's need or satisfy a baby's wish, they are "holding" the baby and promoting the feeling of wellbeing, of being integrated and whole. As Kaplan says, "[The mother] doesn't always have to . . . cuddle him in order to have the experience of being held."

It can't be said too often: meeting a baby's needs creates great confidence in the environment. It is obviously one that provides care in a timely and reliable way and meets expectations. Notice how the physical (being held) shades into the psychological (feeling confident). As the environment consistently satisfies needs, tensions in the baby are kept manageably low, and the baby is all the stronger for it.

The baby's experience of life begins to thicken as human relatedness deepens. Little by little, mother and infant pass imperceptibly into a new relation. The baby leaves the original isolation within the "self" and enters into a symbiosis with the mother.

THE MOTHER-INFANT SYMBIOSIS

In psychology, the meaning of the word symbiosis is not the same as in biology, where it describes an association between two unrelated organisms that benefits both.

For example, there is a bird that feeds on the bits of flesh caught between a crocodile's teeth. The bird walks freely around the teeth of the crocodile, who takes care not to harm the bird: it closes its jaws slowly to warn the bird to fly out to safety. Bird and crocodile enjoy a symbiosis, each meeting its own needs while performing a service for the other.

But symbiosis as used by developmentalists has a narrower meaning: a reciprocal advantage enjoyed by mother and child, two very related beings. On the mother's side the advantage is largely psychological, not physical: even if you prevented a mother from taking care of her baby, she would survive. But to the baby, it is both psychological and physical: without "mothering" (by someone), the baby would die.

But that doesn't begin to describe it. Human symbiosis, from six months to three years, is a long, rich period of caring. It is a love affair between mother and child, and much of what we will talk about is the way it transpires.

THE MOTHER AS EXPERT AND PROTECTOR

During the days just following birth, the mother does what seems right, hoping for the best and watching the baby for confirmation. (In Dr. Spock's famous opening words, "You know more than you think you do.") Nursing and holding the baby comfort both the mother and the infant, helping establish between them an emotional and physical bond. The newborn, sensitive and vulnerable, is still mostly a bundle of reflexes attempting to restore physiology to the earlier "normal" equilibrium, before the "disturbance" of birth.

A few months later, although the baby is in some ways just as vulnerable as at birth, the mother has become proficient in her role of nurturer. She senses more accurately what the baby needs and, comforted by her new knowledge, acts in a more relaxed way. At this point, her mothering feels like a small degree of expertise, and in fact it is.

If necessary, she temporarily skips the satisfaction of her own needs and voluntarily suspends pleasures that can be postponed. Being a new mother, she doesn't mind: the excitement of mothering still hasn't worn off. And also, parents usually agree with the poet Marianne Moore's observation that "You are grown up when you make a sacrifice on behalf of another person and don't call it a sacrifice." But of course what makes this possible for the mother is that she herself once enjoyed a "good enough" symbiosis and developed frustration tolerance.

Prompted by empathy, the mother regresses to the baby's level. That helps her to sense the needs requiring her attention and create a nurturant and secure atmosphere for the baby to discover her as an available partner-in-love. The shift in her hormonal balance, brought on by the changes in her milk-producing breasts (even though she may opt to bottle feed), causes a surge in her nurturing impulses. These induce her to postpone for a time her wish to pursue interests that only recently were absorbing to her—and will soon interest her again.

Sure of her identity, she is developmentally advanced enough to be able to regress to the baby's level. She neither resents nor fears that her selfhood will be lost or swallowed up in the mother-infant relation. Aware that this stage of her baby's growth is relatively brief in the child's life, but developmentally more vital than any later stage, she gives priority to ministering to the baby's needs, knowing it can't work the other way round.

The mother does not worry that her regressing (making high-pitched loving sounds, face peering moonily into the baby's intensely curious face) might rigidify into permanence—though with month-long droughts in adult conversation, the most common joke among new mothers is that their minds show signs of atrophying.

The baby may feel merged with her, but she feels strong enough not to fear merging with the baby. Unlike the baby she has choice. She has attained selfhood and is quite capable of decisions and acting on them. She can regress and come back out of regression. She is also aware that, on the baby's side, this most primitive stage must have its day for it to dissolve itself in the next stage, for which it acts as preparation.

Impelled by the increase in her blood of the hormone prolactin and by a surge of love, she feels moved to accommodate the baby. The baby's helpless, uncoordinated movements appeal to an urge in her to offer protection (pointing up the often overlooked fact that the mother, not the father, is life's first protector).

THE STIMULUS BARRIER

During birthing the baby was impervious to most sensations, and without this protective barrier of insensitivity, birth would indeed have been the trauma that some early theorists claimed.

Even immediately after birth the baby was not very responsive to most stimuli. The larger part of the baby's day was spent neither asleep nor quite awake but in a drowsy, not-quite-conscious continuation of the prenatal state. This state had the effect of protecting against excessive stimuli: the pathways to the sensory apparatus were not fully operative, and their very dullness smoothed over any rough intrusions.

But that has slowly been changing. In recent weeks the baby has become alive and responsive to every passing excitation, poke, light, noise and jolt. The nervous system needs cushioning against the harshness of the world. The month-old baby's body is somewhat better at dealing with mild stimuli, but larger amounts outstrip the baby's ability to deal with them.

The mother becomes a kind of second skin, or a force field around the baby. She reduces stimuli to manageable levels while the baby's inborn screening mechanisms build a protective psychological "rind." Eventually that will take over.

So fundamental is the urge to protect and provide care, especially (but not exclusively) by the mother, that it is observable across species—as true of ducks as it is of elephants and porpoises. The baby's extraordinary neediness evokes in the mother a reciprocal urge to comfort. She intervenes before the baby feels danger, or too great a solitude, or too much discomfort or trouble—too great or too much anything: she regulates, softens, eases, attenuates. And by these means she incidentally creates, from the very beginning, an atmosphere that conveys a quality of life.

THE FIRST SMILES

One indication that the baby is turning from a passive preoccupation with internal stimuli to an active interest in the environment are the first social smiles.

The social smile is not the reflexive, glassy smile occasioned by the baby's digestive contentment, nor is it the involuntary smile during sleep. It is an intentional act.

Directed smiles first appear sometime between the eighth and twelfth weeks, sometimes earlier.

(Figures like these are often given in rough approximation because the term of normal uterine gestation has considerable latitude: "full-term" babies emerge from the uterus after 38 to 42 weeks. That means there can be as much as a whole month of difference in intrauterine growth between two babies born the same day. That spread of a month is reflected in postuterine events.)

The social smile is the second intentional act in life. The first comes around the fifth week, when the baby's eyes track, from a distance, the human face as it moves around the room. At that age, nothing else that the baby looks at produces this response. The tracking is thought to be the forerunner of the baby's relatedness with others. It indicates that the baby's interest has shifted, slightly, from supplies to the bringer of supplies.

The smile is not acquired behavior or a learned response. It is part of our inheritance. And it appears at a particular time because of our biological blueprint: the genes. Genes provide not only the baby's structure but also feelings and behavior, from smiling to running, to sphincter control, to fear of monsters, to wanting to marry Mommy, to playing house and having a baby. Since the blueprint affects behavior over a period of time, we might speak of it as a developmental timetable.

As proof that the appearance of the first smiles is genetically determined, babies who are born blind and never see the human face smile their first social smiles during the second or third month—not before, not after. From this it may be surmised that not just the familiar face but the familiar voice and the in-arms experience—with, possibly, smell and taste contributing—elicit the smile too.

The smile marks the end of the period of the greatest helplessness in human life. The infant has started to function in a voluntary way. When awake, the baby is attentive for longer periods and no longer drifts in and out of sleep but remains more permanently alert to surroundings. The baby (to use Mahler's term) is said to have "hatched."

Another pediatrician-psychoanalyst René Spitz, who, as a member of the Department of Psychiatry of the University of Colorado, directly observed infants in his lifelong study of the first eighteen months of life, made much of this social smile. He described it as a milestone in human development. He said it was the first indication that an internal organization has silently been taking place in the baby.

The smile indicates that perception is no longer a largely visceral experience. The baby is more aware of surroundings than before. With increased neural connections in the brain, thought, in primitive form, is becoming possible.

THE FACE AS CONFIGURATION

The social smile does not mean that the baby is smiling at a human partner. That's an idea whose time has not yet come: there is no human partner. The baby is smiling at a sign. The sign is shaped like a capital T: a configuration of forehead, eyes and nose.

Proof: put a Halloween mask in front of your face, as Spitz did in his famous filmed experiments with three-month-olds, and the baby will beam a smile at the mask because it has the required familiar configuration: forehead, eyes, nose. The baby has an inborn expectation of a certain kind of look, and face and mask are the same.

Spitz extended this experiment. Without a mask, he smiled and looked head on at the baby, and the baby smiled back. Then, holding his smile, Spitz slowly turned his face away so that the baby saw only his profile. The baby stopped smiling and with a puzzled look searched in the vicinity of Spitz's ear for the familiar configuration.

Then Spitz slowly turned his face back, still smiling, and looked at the baby straight on again: the baby's smile reappeared. Spitz concluded that the baby's genetic program for this stage of development recognizes facial features only when they are seen straight on.

Not until the age of six or seven months will the baby become capable of distinguishing the configuration of features as not a sign but a face—a small part of a whole person—and to discriminate one face from all others: a specific person. That highly important advance will signal the completion of another level of development. Spitz said this new change was indicated by "stranger anxiety," or "stranger reactions."

THE DISCOMFORT AT STRANGERS

Though it doesn't sound like it, the term stranger reactions (or sixth- or eighth-month anxiety) points to a favorable development. It is not an indication of something gone wrong. Stranger reactions indicate that the infant has definitely begun to recognize the mother and love her, love her especially. The baby cares deeply to be near her much of the time—in the same way that a baby elephant enjoys being near its mother and a bear cub with its bear mother. Eighth-month anxiety marks the beginning of human relations—relatedness not with a face but with a person.

It may seem to rush chronology to go from the smile at three months to stranger reactions at six, seven or eight months, especially as, in our society, we have become accustomed to reading about cognitive skills, small and large motor development, hand-eye coordination, spatial awareness and socialization skills.

All these are important, but if we are to understand an infant's growing emotions—the baby as a feeling human being—it would be more instructive to focus on love and relatedness than on muscles and skills. Cognitive development doesn't seem so pressing a matter that we need to be aware of its changes month by month: the baby's ability to think grows almost automatically.

And the same with spatial awareness and the acquisition of small-motor skills: even when learning is burdened by emotional handicaps, it is generally true that normal progress in these abilities continues. In fact, it is known that emotional suffering can cause a spurt in learning abilities by the person's sometimes desperate attempt at dealing with suffering. The reverse is not nearly as true: cognitive achievement hardly ever resolves emotional difficulties, though up to a point it can help by bringing understanding to bear.

Childrearing books tend to draw our attention to skills and coordination and seldom speak of babies as darling creatures—in the words of the poet Christopher Morley, "tender elves"—who may also be a drudgery when they don't stop crying or when they wake you up three times in a night. That picture is certainly true. But even when they're being a nuisance they are beautiful human beings, they're enormously appealing and they're happy to give you of themselves freely. The usual descriptions don't include the pure and intense color of their eyes, their mirthful smiles or, in an incredible moment, the first chuckling laugh. All too often books use clinical language—the baby's "advances in the socialization process"—as if experts must write in some sort of officialese. They don't talk about love: they discuss "the baby's attachment behavior." There is often no feeling for the baby as a human being falling in love for the first time and the critical importance of that.

There is no baby without love. There's an empty, hollow shell of a being, barely hanging on to life. There is no growth without love—there is even no life without love. A mother's love is a cohesive force. Mentally and emotionally, her love holds the baby together, feeding the impulse to live, and hope.

The capacity to love is biologically given, but the capacity to feel enduring love is acquired. That's one of the great reasons the baby's beginnings are so important.

Enduring love has one source only: the way the child is nurtured, that is, held, hugged, spoken to lovingly. In adulthood, all relations with others, and especially with a mate, will be modeled unconsciously on this first love and its fate. If love, now, is broken off, or reciprocated inadequately, love in adulthood will easily break off, or inadequate mates will be found. Shallow love in infancy leads to shallow love in adulthood. Inconsistency now means undependability later.

LOVE'S ORAL BEGINNINGS

Like all else in development, love has its stages. In the early months, the infant's love is passive, a "need love." It is a love that takes rather than gives.

The baby is still oral: a haiku observes that

> *the infant,*
> *when shown a flower,*
> *opens his mouth*

In the oral period, everything is "food"—the world is to be ingested. Give the baby a plastic Donald Duck and it goes straight into the mouth. The mouth is still the primary sensing device. Feeling and recognizing things with the hands will come only later. But mouthing the toy also means that the baby loves it and wants to take it inside, make it part of the "me."

The registrations on the psyche, coming together at this supremely impressionable age, are confused—melted together—which is why adult emotional difficulties traceable to the first year have a decidedly oral character: bulimia, anorexia, alcoholism, compensatory overeating, bouts of dieting.

All of these are connected with anger or rage, the emotions produced in the baby by frustrations. They are sometimes called "oral" emotions because they erupt so frequently at the beginning of life. And of course aggressiveness remains in raw form, untamed where there is an insufficiency of love—an insufficiency of meeting the baby's emotional needs.

These symptomatic acts—bulimia, anorexia, alcoholism, overeating, dieting—have a common denominator in the unconscious.

If food is love, then these symptomatic acts are a complication of love. That's one reason that diets notoriously don't work. Diets deal only with food, eating or not eating it, which misses the point. Diets ignore the component of love, for which the food has become a substitute. That's why the need to stuff oneself full followed by the need to starve and lose weight has always been baffling and so stubbornly resistant to change. Conflicting unconscious feelings remain tangled together.

It could probably be shown that those who go through futile cycles of losing and gaining weight were schedule-fed as infants, in a pattern of feeding and going hungry. Or they suffered from some other oral trauma during the first year—a correlation that, by the evidence, holds true of some alcoholics and drug addicts. The huge increase in addiction (including to prescription drugs) in the past half-century may be more than just a coincidence with the widespread custom of scheduled feeding (or premature weaning) and – equally important though less focused on – an insufficient loving closeness of mother and infant.

In this stage, when others are not yet real (the "other" is merely food to be eaten), love consists only of taking for oneself. The infant has begun to emerge (a little) from the state of omnipotence, when there was no awareness of the difference between inside and outside. But the baby is still not much more advanced in development than to perceive others purely as satisfiers of needs.

But love grows and changes in the baby each time one of the baby's needs is met: each satisfaction, as it reduces tensions, is unconsciously translated in the baby's psyche into a sense of all's well. With each pleasure-giving act, the environment tells the baby, "You are wanted and cherished," which joins with the baby's feeling, as Elizabeth Barrett Browning put it:

> *behold me! I am worthy*
> *of thy loving, for I love thee!*

As the infant moves past the initial feelings of life's strangeness, and as needs continue to be satisfied without undue frustration, the baby's liking evolves beyond trust and approval and deepens into love. When the baby sees that the experience of satisfaction is consistent and dependable, the love grows still stronger and gives promise of becoming permanent.

THE PSYCHOLOGICAL MOTHER

Stranger reactions indicate a preference for the mother over others. The preference is egocentric: the mother is still only a mobile extension of the child. Loving her is similar to loving the self.

Still not altogether knowing what is "me" and what is "not me" works in the very young baby's favor. The "goodness" of the environment is taken to be the "goodness" of the baby, part of a healthy self-esteem, which, like love, has its origins very early in life.

There is something special about the mother as part-person: as both self and other. At this age, a Halloween mask would no longer elicit a smile but would make the baby turn away or become tense. Note the shift in needs and in relating.

The same reaction can be seen in the presence of new people, whom the baby notices with marked attention, and even a shrinking back from them. The earlier indifference has become intense discrimination. Discomfort at unfamiliar faces, if they come too close, might make the baby squirm in the mother's arms, or cry and whimper—or just grow quietly watchful. Or the baby may shyly twist the head away and burrow into the mother's shoulder.

If looking at objects internalizes them as part of the self, then, in the baby's logic, not looking at them gets rid of them. That is one of the earliest expressions of the defense called denial: turn your head away and "disappear" what bothers you and it no longer exists.

Now there begins to be keenness in the sorrow at being forcibly separated from this dependable, smiling part-person. Where love is strong, there is inconsolable sadness at losing the loved one. It affects the baby the same way it affects all lovers: with a loss of appetite, sleeplessness, a refusal to be comforted by anyone else. ("Only one person is lacking, and the whole world feels empty," the French poet Lamartine said.) "Feeding problems" in the early months are nearly always emotional in origin. They are the expression of the baby's feelings about the special other and the "loss" of that person.

One of the most harmful things parents can do when the baby is around six months old is to go off on a trip and leave the baby with family, or with a caretaker. The parents may need a break at this point—all parents do—but this is precisely the age when the baby smiles happily at their sight and is falling in love with them more deeply than ever and feeling something like "life is wonderful." Suddenly that whole beautifully evolving world falls apart. Two-thirds of the primal triad of mother-father-baby disappears: the baby wakes up from a nap, and no parents—especially no Mommy. The child feels utterly alone. And a psychologically unseparated child feeling alone ceases to exist. The baby has a feeling of deadness, of unspeakable despair.*

---

* Older babies and toddlers feel this too, and are capable of articulating it. Once, when the mother and father of a three-year-old boy were sent to prison, the child was asked by a psychiatrist: "When a baby is separated from his mother, the baby is lost, isn't he?" The boy answered: "No, the baby is dead."

This is true if the parents go away "only" overnight, as they might view it, and is far worse if they're gone for a weekend (or longer: a month-long vacation would be devastating).

The baby's sorrow at this special other's disappearance means that childrearing is going well. The "other" has begun to be valued. That is a significant advance in the baby's relations with people. For the first three months, where no one face was more familiar or loved than another, anyone could have been the mother. But from now on, the mother is no longer interchangeable. She is a specific person, and the baby's first feelings of love have become attached to her. She has become the child's psychological mother.

OF BABY WHALES, AND LOVE AND DEATH

We sometimes read of orphaned baby whales languishing without their mother and her energizing presence even though concerned marine biologists devote round-the-clock care for the great babies. But no amount of stroking their backs or feeding them fish emulsion mixed with vitamins or swimming in the tank alongside them and making whale sounds makes baby whales feel loved. It sometimes happens that by accident these gigantic baby mammals fasten their mouth on the index finger of a marine biologist and suck it as if it were their mother's nipple—forlorn hope. The behavior of the baby whales calls to mind the hospitalized babies that the pediatrician René Spitz had studied. Having lost their mothers, they lay supine in their cribs, no longer caring to sit up anymore and becoming unfeeling creatures, indifferent to those around them. Orphaned newborn whales behave similarly, and more often than not, they give up and die.

THE DOLL OR TOY AS A TRANSITION

An outward sign that differentiation is increasing is the baby's settling on a doll or a stuffed animal, or even a blanket, as a favorite object. From one day to the next, no other object will do for hugging and carrying around.

The need for the mother's body, as the psychiatrist Phyllis Greenacre said, is

> *touchingly expressed in the infant's insistent preference for an object which is lasting, soft, pliable, warm to the touch.... The fact that the object is usually pressed against the face close to the nose probably indicates how well it substitutes for the mother's breast or soft neck.*

Starting now and continuing for many years, baby and doll, or baby and security blanket, become inseparable. A rubber nipple, or "dummy" plays the same role.

Winnicott called the doll or blanket the "transitional object." In a culture in which the infant is not carried on the mother's "person" at all times, the doll substitutes for her. The adoption of the transitional object means the infant has begun to accept the reality that mother and baby are physically separate. The doll acts as emotional support and makes the separation from the mother tolerable. It is one more sign that things are going well.

THE "CUSTOMS INSPECTOR"

The infant who, in the first six months, has become familiar with a particular person will not want to be left alone without that person now. An unfamiliar face might take the baby away from the familiar one—mother. Having fallen in love with the mother, the baby has a new fear: losing her. This is a good sign, one that means all is going well.

If you leave the baby alone with a stranger you give the baby a problem to solve: how to deal with the stranger and still feel safe—if that's possible. It's a dilemma, and the baby does not have the means for resolving dilemmas.

No half-year-old baby is accustomed to the idea that problems and difficulties are a normal part of life. Ordinarily, when problems present themselves, they require thought before answers can be found. But in the baby, thought is murky, and besides, the whole thing is too complicated and perplexing and far too premature for the six-month-old mind. And whatever happens prematurely for a given emotional age is for that reason traumatic.

The strange still feels unsettling, and starting now and extending into the second year, it is not surprising that the baby carefully scrutinizes all new faces. All curiosity and a vivid interest in surroundings grow keen, but curiosity about strangers runs particularly strong. You can easily observe this "custom's inspection" when you and your baby are with someone that the baby is seeing for the very first time. The baby stares so long and hard at the unfamiliar face that you sometimes get the impression that the features are being committed to memory.

THE BABY'S INCREASING PERCEPTION

Love begins at the breast, in the enjoyment of feedings. The baby's lips and gums stimulate the nipples that provide the milk. Some mother's say the physical pleasure borders on sexual arousal and sometimes passes over into it. They have been known to have an orgasm while breastfeeding, and of course that is perfectly normal. (Others, it should be pointed out, suffer sore nipples and a sense of failure at breastfeeding – feelings that usually fade with experience.)

And it is not uncommon for a new breastfeeding mother, brimming with contentment and stirred by her affectionate contact with the baby, to lose interest, for a time, in making love with her husband. To make love with a mate has its special pleasures but they can wait. Mother and infant meet in a private world, and for now, there is something inexpressibly more satisfying in nurturing the baby that is not the same as making love with the baby's father. The father understands that the two experiences are different and the changes temporary, and his maturity helps him overcome any resentment at "being left out."

The baby's contented feeding is accompanied by a steady upward gazing at the mother's (or nurturer's) face. "Love comes in at the eye," Yeats said. Relations grow stronger as baby and feeder regard each other with a quiet contentment. The baby blends into one these simultaneous activities:

drinking the milk and studying the face of the milk provider. As the mouth takes in the milk, the eyes take in the person. From such beginnings, contact perception shades into distance perception.

The Whatever, the Out There, gradually transforms itself into individual things. Each thing possesses an identifying appearance, or sound, or feel. And at the same time, coming in and around and through these experiences are glimmerings of "the other": hints that mother and baby too have individual looks and feelings—and the conviction grows even more that mother and baby are separate beings.

With distance perception, the baby can view objects across the room. Seeing reveals more of reality than touching did: a glance takes in the visible world. Touching could not do that. As seeing bridges distance, the environment fills in more rapidly than ever.

180-DEGREE TURNS
Individual things don't yet make sense, not always, but they are definitely not some hallucination, something happening purely in the baby's mind.

The baby learns this by doing an experiment. It happens one day, around the third or fourth month, unexpectedly. Nothing alerts the observer of its approach The baby swings the head around, and all the objects the baby was looking at disappear. The baby swings the head back—and the objects reappear.

The baby does what a scientist would do: applies the test several times. The result is always the same. The baby seems to understand: if things were merely imaginings, then it wouldn't matter where the eyes looked. The objects would still be visible. Conclusion, therefore: the Out There exists independently of the baby's imagination. It's quite a feat of thought.

This fascinating discovery is a major step in establishing that there are two worlds: the inside world and the outside world. Both are much alike. The physical one outside is incontestably real. The one inside is just as real, but as perceptions and imaginings. This marvelous new distinction reinforces the growing sense of identity: inside is me, outside is not-me.

It is striking that the profoundest questions in life are precisely those we ask at the beginning of life, and though the answers get refined, they never change. The baby's discovery of "thereness" extends into adulthood as a concern with the fundamental questions of philosophy: "What is out there?" "Why is there something instead of nothing?" Philosophy asks simple questions like "What's it all about?" which is the very same question the baby asks, though the baby doesn't have the language in which to frame it. It will take the baby half a lifetime or more to find out that philosophers don't have the language either.

GROWING RELATEDNESS

With love focused on the mother and with mother increasingly becoming a physically separate person, the possibility of losing her becomes a real threat to the baby. Closeness, the baby can't help feeling, is the surest safeguard against loss.

The smiling response was the first clear-cut indication of attachment. But in that foggy earlier time, needs were paramount—were alone real. People had no importance as people and could come and go as long as the baby's needs were met.

In fact, for practically the whole of the first three years of an infant's life, "relationship" is a way of saying "gratify my needs." Satisfying the baby is the be-all and end-all of the face, the "other," the slowly clarifying Whatever. The world owes the infant a living, a feeling that is valid and normal at this stage.

We know that "mother" could be anyone—for a brief time, several anyones: a father, a mother, an uncle, an older sibling, even, perhaps, according to accounts of infants raised by wolves, an animal. To the undifferentiated baby, there is only the experience of nurture.

Even if the biological mother should be absent from the child's daily life, her functions are taken over by other caregivers. The child who is not cared for, touched, fed and played with by the mother herself is thus cared for, touched, fed and played with by others. To the baby these others are "Mother."

Development is in part the formation in the baby of the idea of the mother—and of the self, and of the father, and of other figures: in brief, of human relatedness.

It is only slowly that the need gratifier becomes "the mother." It's the person the baby perceives to be the most consistent nurturer. Nearly always and in nearly all cultures, that is the biological mother. But even if it's the father, to the baby he plays the role of mother. The baby knows nothing of gender or role.*

---

* Coney Island Hospital, in New York, reported that a 41-year-old transvestite father, wanting equality with his wife in the breastfeeding of their baby daughter, was given injections of prolactin, the hormone normally secreted by the pituitary gland. Prolactin produces not just milk in the breasts but feelings of maternal love (virgin animals injected with prolactin begin to mother). The father became "maternal," as

much the infant's breastfeeding mother as his wife was. Father and mother alternately nursed the baby for six to eight months. The baby accepted the milk of both as though that were normal, which to her it was.

THE MOTHER WITHIN THE BABY

The idea "mother" grows inside the baby. The baby internalizes the mother in a series of mental images.

But instead of images it would be more accurate to employ the term used by the psychoanalyst Edith Jacobson and speak of mental representations. Image suggests only looks and appearances. Representation includes also the mother's voice, smell, feel, warmth, strength, gestures, clothing and even the space she moves in. She is the sum of sensory impressions and thought associated with her. She is a sphere of activity—a devoted concern. All these the baby takes inside and they become "Mother."

Creating this inner mother is what will eventually make independence feasible. It is having the mother firmly inside that will make it possible to let go of the flesh-and-blood outside mother.

THE WHOLE MOTHER: BOTH "GOOD" AND "BAD"

Because the baby's pleasurable experiences feel dependable, and because they (through good-enough nurturing) outnumber the unpleasurable ones, the baby's love grows stronger and stronger. And something else happens too.

For quite some time the baby, differentiating from the mother, has been misperceiving her almost as though she were two mothers: one is the mother who meets needs—the "good mother."

Unfortunately the idea of the "good mother" does not account for the baby's pains and frustrations. A "good mother" would not cause or allow such terrible experiences but would prevent them. Therefore, in the baby's logic, there must also be a "bad mother." It is the bad mother who is responsible for failing to bring needed satisfactions, for frustrations, for allowing the baby to suffer. She is to be hated (and also, incidentally—for that very reason—feared).

Now, though, as perception reads reality more clearly, the baby becomes dimly aware that the bad mother and the good mother are actually one person. That may be obvious to us, but the thought is novel to the baby. There isn't a gratifying mother who unpredictably becomes a horrible monster who frustrates. There is a whole-person mother. She is the "good" and the "bad" mother rolled into one.

This unifies an unconscious split picture of her and makes her a more real person: she is a human being. She begins slowly to be seen as someone who meets needs but occasionally gets distracted and forgets, who both frustrates and gratifies, who doesn't always know what she's doing, who is sometimes very good at things and sometimes falls down on the job completely—the gamut. But most of all, she is devoted to the baby: the baby notes that and likes it—and tries to be "devoted" to her.

A cultural residue of the very young infant's split of "good mother" and "bad mother" is preserved in the legends of all cultures: the tales of the fairy godmother and the horrible witch queen, and stories involving genies and demons. It is amusing to adults to see the fervor with which very young children believe these Grand Guignol tales. Frightening adults are still quite real to them and so is the terror they inspire, evidence that infantile misperceptions have by no means been outgrown. Even in adulthood, where childhood emotional difficulties remain unresolved, monsters and terrifying figures show up in anxiety dreams.

UNCOMPLIANCE AND THE EMERGING SELF

To develop a relation between the self and another requires that there first be a self. The most obvious "self" the infant has is the body.

The existence of another being begins to be obvious when the baby notices that the breast periodically disappears. The breast has to be something apart from the infant's body and sensations: the infant's body and sensations are always present, but the breast is not.

As we saw earlier, what helps to convince the baby are small amounts of frustration happening naturally and unavoidably. Between a need and the provision of supplies is a gap, and the gap hints at separateness.

This new sense of separateness excites the imagination. In a push to learn, everything that emphasizes difference is used to test that notion. Acrobatic deep-knee bends in the mother's lap, arching away from her chest and rearing back to view her from a new perspective as both feet push against her abdomen—these are good exercises for maturing arm and leg muscles. But they are also the lap baby's attempts at feeling different distances from the mother, as though to confirm the decrease in bodily dependence on her.

The baby energetically lunges at the mother's nose, grabs at her hair and at the same time shoves mightily away from her face, to see how those experiences feel. The mother holds the baby's body securely while allowing freedom for the gymnastics to be enjoyed, and that builds in the baby the sense of two opposing though not necessarily antagonistic wills. The difference in wills becomes further proof that the self and the other are different.

These characteristic acts, which every parent recognizes, are genetically determined. They come from the aggressive vigor of developmental force, not the aggression of hostility. That means that aggression can have a positive connotation—it doesn't necessarily mean hate or destructiveness. It refers to the (psychic) energy that powers development. It's the aggressive energy we touched on earlier, the developmental energy that becomes available when aggressiveness has been tamed, or harnessed, and become available for use.

Viewed this way, certain approaching changes in development—contrariness and temper tantrums, for example (and, a few years later, adolescent rebelliousness)—make sense. They are not "problems," not in themselves. The thrust behind a child's (and an adolescent's) explosions of anger and hate becomes clear. The emotions may be urgently, bluntly, incoherently expressed, and they may test the limits of parents' endurance, but they blow over: they are developmental thrusts and indicate progress in development.

Not to comply in all ways is a sign of health. It is an assertion of selfhood. The aggression in noncompliance fosters separation and builds autonomy. And if any one thing can be said to be the goal of childrearing it's the building of autonomy.

For now, around the middle of the first year, the main push of aggressive energy is in differentiating as much as possible the self from what is not the self.

The baby knows that the crying voice is part of the "me." So are the sensations inside the body. And so too the tiny hands that wave in and out of the field of vision—and the satin mucosity of fingers in mouth—and many other increasingly familiar experiences besides.

Though the mother's nipple and the baby's fingers both go into the mouth, the sensations in the fingers are different—and they are available always. The baby acquires special emotions about them—possessiveness, for one. The baby naturally loves the body: the body is "me" and the "me" experience is for the most part a pleasurable one and therefore it is good: what is good can be loved. "' I ' can be loved."

And the "me" is special. The toes can go into the mouth just like the mother's cheek can (or as the mother's cheek almost can). But to touch and taste the toes has one feeling, and to touch and taste the mother's cheek has a different feeling. For one thing, the baby feels the sensation in both mouth and toe. And the same goes for the baby's skin when it is being caressed and soaped and washed during a bath.

Learning Boundaries

At around this age—the second half of the first year—all mothers notice that the baby's aggressiveness increases. The lap baby becomes physically more energetic, more playful, painfully yanking a lock of the mother's hair and nearly gouging her eyes out with sharp-nailed fingers. These are not attacks—there's no malice or anger—but clumsy explorations. Small-muscle skills have a considerable way to go yet. The explorations continue to confirm the boundaries of the self and the touchable separateness of baby and mother.

The baby needs to repeat the experience. The endless rediscovery that there is the self and there is also the other becomes a subject for long-term observation. Even well into the second year the baby will go on testing the fascinating differences between self and other—as when the mother offers the baby her breast or the bottle and the baby simultaneously crams a handful of tiny fingers between her lips and twiddles them: the baby is "feeding" the mother. That's an indication that the mother feeding the baby and the baby feeding the mother are not yet altogether two different experiences but one: mother and baby are having a feeding.

During a spoon-feeding the baby might insist on having a private spoon. A spoon of one's own is good for more than just the loud banging noises it so satisfyingly produces (a scientific lesson in itself: on the nature of the world as sounds, surfaces, volumes and percussiveness). The baby wants to have a spoon for the same reason that the mother has a spoon: to offer a feeding.

Mothers take this "feeding the mother" to be an early sign of generosity—an adult notion that doesn't match the infant's stage of development. These same mothers are then dismayed, at around the beginning of the third year, by the infant's sudden "selfishness" at wanting to hold on to everything as "Mine!" This is the mistake of adultomorphism—reading adult meanings into the baby's acts. Adulthood and its rules are still light-years away.

The selfishness, so called, is progress. When the baby grows into a possessive being and wants to hold onto everything, it demonstrates that differentiation of the me from the other has become quite pronounced. Once the baby understands the boundaries of the self, the philosophy of "what's mine is mine" is adopted with a passion. The humbling erosion of omnipotence creates a need for compensation, and any opportunity for self-aggrandizement is seized on.

Having only an incomplete sense of self, the baby is willing to try anything as part of the process of self-discovery and becoming. Mimicry, which comes shortly before the ability to speak is achieved, is the infant's first way of learning to feel others' attitudes and moods. You can see outmoded traces of this behavior in adulthood when a listener, moved by another's speech, involuntarily makes the same grimaces and lip movements the speaker is making. And parents—sometimes especially fathers—open their mouths as the spoon approaches the baby's.

Babyloving

Imitating and learning the mother's attitude help ensure the success of a relationship with her. If you know your supplier and do the things that please, your needs will have a better chance of being met. Where they feel loved, infants are naturally cooperative. And they expect adults to conduct themselves cooperatively too.

The wish for the original mother-infant oneness does not fade easily. Couples making love sometimes experience an odd sense of being a single person. An early unsatisfied need for symbiosis peeks through this desire to obliterate separation. It calls to mind Plato's theory of love: we fall in love because the two halves of a person are going through life searching for each other in order to restore an earlier oneness. The French philosopher Rousseau, whose mother died within a day or two of his birth, gives clear expression in his Confessions to the yearning for union:

> *The first of my wants, the greatest, the strongest, and most insatiable, was wholly in my heart; the want of an intimate connection, and as intimate as it could possibly be. . . . This singular want was such, that the closest corporal union was not sufficient: two souls would have been necessary to me in the same body, without which I always felt a void.*

NONVERBAL LANGUAGE AND EARLY HUMAN RELATIONS

As the mother's love becomes increasingly valued, the baby wants the assurance that her love will not waver. When the mother sounds irritated, or if some passing thought (a bill to be paid, news of family illness) should cause her to frown, the baby becomes anxious. Does it mean a break in her love?

And if so, what occasioned it? To feel safe again, the baby makes an effort to elicit signs of affection from her. Some mothers say they notice in their twelve-month-old baby a visible appreciation of them.

They sometimes also observe, mixed with the gratitude, a need to propitiate the mother, as if the baby had just found out which side the bread is buttered on. Mothers who catch this look say the baby seems almost wisely self-protective, in this respect almost clever.

The emotional closeness to her and physical dependence on her, now more apparent to the baby, are helped by the development of verbal communication. Vocalization and speech make for still greater closeness. The sound of the human voice creates a sense of closeness—as expressed one night by a slightly older child to his mother on being put to bed: "It's not so dark when I can hear your voice."

All through the second half of the first year, the baby, in a spirited attempt at language, has begun to command an impressive gibberish. To adults it may seem like nonsensical groupings of syllables, but to the infant they are earnest communications. The attempts do not always mean to convey anything in particular but are often the baby's way of sounding like others. Babies understand feelings more than words, and sometimes they want to convey their feelings to you, and when they go on and on with what to parents are meaningless sounds, it's as though they were engaging them in a dialogue.

As speech shades into semantic communication, the baby employs a range of means to express needs: looks, squirms and arm and leg movements, and, lately, a variety of sounds. The mother responds selectively. Where she understands the need, she supplies it. The baby picks up on her selectivity by noticing which efforts lead to the desired responses.

Through a long experience, the baby learns with accuracy how to effect results and makes them part of the vocabulary of the mother-infant "language." Each empathically reads the other's signals and learns to accommodate the other more smoothly. The communications are pragmatic: found to be true when tested by consequences.

The infant's method of having needs met will in a couple of years lead to a code of ethics—to note in passing how early in life the sense of ethics begins. The baby understands, however fuzzily, that the provider of satisfactions is a person. She is not merely a gratifier of needs, to be dismissed when her services are no longer needed, like a waiter in a restaurant once the meal has been served.

That narcissistic, premoral view of the other begins now to be left behind. Ever more clearly perceiving that needed satisfactions come from an outside source that is dependable and loving, the baby gladly cooperates and tries to treat the other well. Even before there's language, before walking even, the value of ethics in human relations comes to life.

Unlike biological birth, which is a dramatic and observable event, the slow unfolding of psychological gestation and psychological birth is an intrapsychic event—it is an internal event—requiring thirty-six months to complete.

Gestation is made up of three parts: biology, psychology and the environment.

The biology is self-regulating. It maintains our life without our being conscious of it. Neither our wishes nor our customs can influence biology. Will power can't deflect it from its course. It has the hardiness of millions of years of evolution. It is not surprising that, especially at the beginning of life, biology is more powerful than either psychology or the environment: life is, first and last, survival.

Psychology is inborn also. Babies—Polynesian, Amazonian, Navajo—develop alike during the first two or three months whatever form parenting takes. The baby born at the gestational age of forty-two weeks will, during the second month of infancy, begin to smile. By the sixth or seventh month, the baby will show signs of stranger reactions, and at around fifteen months will go through a period of feeling contrary. We know from the careful studies of the Swiss psychologist Jean Piaget that it doesn't matter what the baby's previous experience or constitutional endowment is. Acquiring certain abilities follows an invariable course in all children in all cultures. A given ability's outward expression may vary from one culture to another. But the abilities themselves don't.

The third component, the environment, in the early months means the parents, or the nurturing experience.

The three—biology, psychology and environment—work in harmony.

PSYCHOLOGY: VULNERABLE TO INFLUENCE

Biology is resolute and unyielding. It is much tougher than psychology. Compared with it, psychological development is susceptible to all sorts of pressures.

That has a benign side: the environment—the parents—play a significant role in childrearing by facilitating development. They ease it along and influence it.

As an example: somewhere around the end of the first year, every baby feels an urge to stand up and walk unaided. Biology and psychology work together: the quarter million genes in a baby's chromosomes (biology) provide the "walking code," so to speak. At the same time, when the baby performs the balancing act of placing one foot in front of the other and moving forward without support, it comes out of an urge or desire to do so (psychology). How does the environment influence the two? By providing an atmosphere of emotional support and love from the beginning. That instills in the baby a contentment at being alive and the courage to try.

Development can be hindered also, usually unintentionally. We can learn what not to do from dramatic examples of emotional neglect. Spitz described a group of unfortunate babies who felt unloved and unsupported. They had been taken from their mothers at the age of six months and we can guess that they felt something like abandonment. Observers said they looked only half-alive. Hospital staff members, providing complete care in the way of food, medical attention and hygiene, were surprised to find that when the babies reached the age when they could be expected to creep and then walk, many of them withdrew to a corner of the crib and, lying like rag dolls, showed no signs even of wanting to sit up. They lost weight, stopped smiling, shrank from strange faces and languished where they lay. They grew apathetic and stared into space, or for long stretches made bizarre, senseless movements with their hands.

Encouragement—being picked up and held and hugged—was lacking (the environmental factor). And so the psychological component suffered: the infants had no wish to do anything. They showed barely any response to their being kept clean and fed. Yet biologically they were at an age when creeping and then walking was possible.

Spitz commented that the babies did not even feel sorrow at the frequent disappearances of their caregivers: the nurses could come and go—night shift, day shift, it didn't matter. If one nurse went on vacation, another was just as acceptable, and emotionally just as meaningless. Everyone had equal value—that is, no value. These babies had never been given the opportunity to become attached to one specific person, a principal caregiver who would become valued.

Whatever feeling of love remained in them gave the impression of being a fearful love. They showed stronger ties with the inanimate environment, which is understandable: the objects around them were their most constant companion. It was almost as if they were escaping inner conflict by giving up on people. That was emotionally safer, though paradoxically it led to their death: hardly any reached the age of one. The psychiatrist Selma Fraiberg commented on Spitz's study: "The motion picture made of these mute, solemn children, lying stuporous in their cribs, is one of the little-known horror films of our time."

SAD EXPERIMENTS PROVIDED BY FATE

Fortunately such extreme cases are rare—but they are not unique. Similarly instructive is the account by the historian Salimbene, a thirteenth-century Italian Franciscan friar, who recorded an experiment by the Holy Roman Emperor Frederick II (1194-1250), who, because of his learning, was called "Stupor Mundi" (wonder of the world).

The emperor was curious to know what language children would spontaneously speak if, from birth onward, no word was spoken in their presence. Would it be a classical tongue, like Hebrew, Greek or Latin, or a contemporary language, like Arabic or German?

He instructed the nurses of these orphans to breastfeed and bathe them and see to their material needs but never to speak to them. The conditions of the experiment were similar to those of Spitz's study, except that these babies—so far as is known—had not first had loving care before being deprived.

But the results were identical. Despite adequate physical care, none of the babies "cooperated" with the language experiment but gave up on the human race and died. Salimbene, who recorded their sad fate, perceived the importance of closeness and warm human contact and understood what had happened. Being fed and bathed and kept warm satisfied their material needs, but the emotional needs went starving. "They could not live without the petting and joyful faces and loving words of their foster mothers."

And there are documented cases of infants in Iranian orphanages raised without much attention during their earliest months: those not adopted by the age of two showed signs of retarded functioning in adolescence. And it is common knowledge that institutionalized babies not placed in foster homes until their second or third year have difficulty forming stable human bonds.

"OLD ANNA" AND LOVING CARE

This interplay of environment (the parents) and psychology (the baby's feeling-needs—the baby's innate expectations) seemed to Margaret Mahler, the psychoanalyst and authority on child development, insufficiently appreciated. During her student days in Vienna, she observed babies "boarded" in sterilized glass-walled cubicles and fed through nipples inserted into the walls so that there would be no physical contact with the infants because that was thought to be "best" for them. We are horrified today to read of such treatment of babies, but in the early days of the twentieth century that was considered "healthy care", with the emphasis on health. "Health" seemed to have the narrow definition of "germ free." It is not surprising that those babies who survived fared poorly.

Another observer, the anthropologist Ashley Montagu, mentioned earlier, said that during the nineteenth century more than half of the infants hospitalized in their first year of life regularly died from a disease called infantile debility, or marasmus, a Greek word meaning "wasting away." According to Montagu:

> *As late as the second decade of the twentieth century the death rate for*

infants under one year of age in various foundling institutions throughout the United States was nearly 100 percent! It was Dr. Henry Dwight Chapin, the distinguished New York pediatrician, who, recognizing the emotional aridity of the children's institutions, introduced into America the system of boarding out babies instead of leaving them in institutions. But it was Dr. Fritz Talbot of Boston who brought the idea of "Tender, Loving Care," not in so many words but in practice, back with him from Germany, which he had visited before World War I. While in Germany Dr. Talbot called at the Children's Clinic in Düsseldorf, where he was shown over the wards by Dr. Arthur Schlossmann, the director. The wards were very neat and tidy, but what piqued Dr. Talbot's curiosity was the sight of a fat old woman who was carrying a very measly baby on her hip. "Who's that?" inquired Dr. Talbot. "Oh, that," replied Schlossmann, "is Old Anna. When we have done everything we can medically for a baby, and it is still not doing well, we turn it over to Old Anna, and she is always successful.

Montagu quotes Dr. James L. Halliday, the author of Psychosocial Medicine:

> *The absence of accustomed mother contact has a bearing on the problem of "fretting" such as is seen when an infant is removed from a hospital. Many of us who have been resident medical officers in a fever hospital used to be somewhat skeptical of the importance of fretting, but recent observations have shown its reality and its practical importance, in that infants deprived of their accustomed maternal body contact may develop a profound depression with lack of appetite, wasting, and even marasmus leading to death. As a result of these findings volunteer women now attend some of the children's hospitals to provide infants that are fretting with periods of handling, caressing, rocking, etc. (The results are said to be dramatic.)*

Montagu also mentions that a

> Dr. J. Brennemann [starting in the late 1920s] established the rule in his hospital that every baby should be picked up, carried around, and "mothered" several times a day. At Bellevue Hospital in New York,

> following the institution of
> "mothering" on the pediatric wards,
> the mortality rates for infants under
> one year fell from 30 to 35 percent
> to less than 10 percent by 1938.

Even if we agree that these are not examples of everyday mothering, they point up how emotionally dependent babies are on close and consistent nurturing during their first year, and that's worth learning. The mother who enjoys being a mother is like Old Anna, whose "secret technique" was that she loved nurturing babies. She felt in her bones what all psychotherapists know: babies don't need qualified, conscientious personnel, or the right staff-child ratio, or advanced medical programs in sanitary settings. The mothering environment must have a human quality, not mechanical perfection. It is this human quality that lays down the basis for "mental health," as it has been called, or emotional stability, which is what is meant. And the mothering person must be consistent, that is, the same person.

Qualified personnel, medical programs and sanitary settings are generally thought of as "children's rights." But that is an institutional view of babies. By themselves these rights, so called, though they show concern, don't provide nearly enough. They leave out babies as human individuals-in-the-making and having human needs, and the greatest need is for down-home love, in-arms contact, and rocking and talking. And that was what Old Anna supplied.

In her memoirs, Margaret Mahler spoke of marasmic babies whose lives were saved by "compassionate and dedicated student nurses" who carried the babies around "day and night, 'loving' them out of the worst doldrums." The babies "emerged out of their comatose, toxic states, their diarrhea stopped, and in most cases, they slowly became well." In contrast, in a similar institute on the other side of

Vienna, babies exactly like them died in large numbers despite medical attention. The difference, she said, was "the human ingredient of loving care."

Again and again we see how important a part love plays in the development of a human being. What makes this worth stressing is that the ability to provide loving care does not come automatically. It takes time to actually love a baby. For one thing, expectant mothers speak of their curiosity to see what their baby will look like and are often surprised by the real baby's face because it is not the way they imagined it. And for another, some mothers dislike having a baby, usually for reasons of their own upbringing. Apart from that, not all women have a maternal instinct (by whatever name we choose to call the nurturing impulse).

Having a child doesn't make a mother. If a mother doesn't want to do mothering or actually hates having a baby and wishes "it" had never been born, both mother and child would benefit by letting someone else do the mothering.

TO SEPARATE AND BECOME AN INDIVIDUAL

The baby's psychological development progresses on a double track. One track is psychologically separating from the mother. The other track is becoming an individual.

Evolving as an individual, a baby develops all the emotional tendencies, quirks and traits (many of which are inborn) that make each person different.

Then there's the other track, psychological separation. Psychological separation leads to the baby's belief, finally, that the self and the other are completely separate beings, not just physically but in every possible way.

Before, the idea of separate existences was suspected—and it was unconsciously fought. Now, it begins to be a conviction.

This two-tracked process extends from about the middle of the first year to thirty-six months and beyond.

Along the way, the infant evolves from a mostly biological organism to a person with a unique identity.

At the same time, dependence evolves into independence. And symbiosis grows into autonomy.

These are large and important developments and "mental health" (emotional maturity and wellbeing) depends on them.

Margaret Mahler outlined four phases of development leading to psychological separation:

First phase: the baby learns there are boundaries (there's the self and there's the mother). This is called differentiation (from around the fifth to the ninth month—as the baby advances from crawler to almost toddler).

Second phase: the baby leaves the mother's side for exciting forays into the other-than-mother world as the baby learns to toddle and then walk. This "practicing" phase extends roughly from nine to fourteen months.

Third phase: the toddler feels a wish for what Mahler called rapprochement with the mother, meaning renewed closeness with her. This phase surprises parents, who almost always misinterpret it to mean that their child has begun regressing and somehow it's the fault of their childrearing.

Admittedly that looks like regression to an earlier dependence on her but it isn't. In this new phase the truth has begun to sink in, deeply and permanently, that the mother really is separate. The knowledge can no longer be fought off. The mother has a life of her own and interests that exclude the child.

The dawning awareness of this comes as an extremely hard blow to the child. The toddler, until now never having felt excluded by the mother, reaches out to her. That's what makes this not a regression and different from earlier. Back then, the infant passively accepted her love. Now, the toddler takes the initiative and asks for closeness. Obviously that is progress, and it is in the direction of autonomy, which is always to the good.

Fourth phase: the "senior" toddler attains "object constancy." The child's mental representations of the mother have been internalized enduringly. They no longer easily fade with time. The mother is now carried around inside the child in a permanent way, even when she is—for the moment—hated (for example, because of an argument).

Nature never rushes development. Changes are lasting and solidly based when they proceed not in fits and starts but in an atmosphere of calm. The reality of separateness is best assimilated gradually.

The gradualness has importance: some "omnipotence" is still necessary for the enjoyment of living. Even though it must eventually be given up, ideally it is relinquished through a slow wearing away. That allows the child time to get used to living without its emotional support. In contrast, when a belief in omnipotence suddenly collapses it traumatizes. Early in life there is such a thing as an overdose of reality.

The child's awareness of vulnerability is one of the principal reasons why brief separations from the mother can cause anxiety. Separation can stir to life the fear of abandonment. To an observer, the degree of anxiety aroused in a toddler may appear too small to be serious. But (to recall Rousseau's urging us to "see, think and feel" as children do) to the child the anxiety is very real and it is heartbreaking. In such moments even familiar adults are not easily tolerated as substitutes for the mother, which is not surprising: how could they allay the child's anxiety when it is precisely their presence instead of the mother's that is the cause of the anxiety?

In the earliest months it was different. Then surrogates could replace the mother—as long as they provided nurture and care. Now, separations from the mother can hurt, and badly. Not just needs are real but she is real. And the need to love her and feel loved by her is real too. So ardently is continued closeness needed during the rapprochement phase that tears at unwanted separations are the rule.

At this age, the third year of life, children are capable of complaining verbally. They don't just whine or burst into tears. But sometimes too, the complaint is expressed through actions. If the mother, ignoring the toddler's cue, fails to involve herself with the child, the child might hit whatever is claiming her attention: a magazine she is reading or the telephone if she is making a call. If these means of involving her do not get the message across, the baby might furiously smash an object on the floor or pound the rug and scream, with eyes peripherally watching the mother and ears listening for her response.

So crucial to development is this increased need for closeness, this need for rapprochement, that if it is persistently ignored ("so as not to spoil the child by catering to every whim") it can cause painful disappointment in the child's feelings toward the mother. That, not so incidentally, is one of the sources of depression in adulthood.

Depression doesn't announce itself in its adult form when it first begins. One childhood sign of it is a tendency to cry easily. Another is a low-keyed searching-for-mother behavior. Or sometimes just the reverse: pointedly ignoring the mother or turning away from her. These could indicate trouble ahead, perhaps not until adulthood.

Sometimes when the child turns away and prefers to be alone, or away from home, some mothers (fathers too) seize on it as the respite from parenting they've been yearning for. Unfortunately they ignore that it means the child is disappointed in them. The "indifference," if it lasts more than a brief spell (an hour or two, certainly a day or more), is a disruption in affection for them, a break in the child's love, which could have eventual unpleasant consequences. Their ignoring it of course only worsens the condition.

Before psychological birth – which won't come until the baby is thirty-six months old – sorrow at separation doesn't mean that development has gone wrong. It means the reverse: it means that love has grown stronger. Its very strength is a sign that the other is more than ever valued, and the child wants the parent to understand that. The child wants the parent to be glad of the depth of the love and its being freely offered, and wants the love to be welcomed as the pleasurable experience the child feels it is.

The love of parent and child for one another is, after all, one of the most fulfilling experiences in life, and the toddler who looks to have the need for closeness warmly reciprocated would be hurt and shocked if it is not. The child's scale of values is in this respect unimprovable. The wish for closeness is a sign of great emotional development in the toddler, who expects, believes and assumes the parents to be no less developed.

FATHER AND SEPARATION

The relations with the father grow rapidly during the practicing and rapprochement phases.

It is a curious fact that many prospective fathers don't give themselves the credit they deserve (the same, incidentally, can be said about many mothers too). They feel intimidated by fatherhood and inadequate to the task.

Actually most fathers are developmentally more mature than they think they are and soon find how easy it is to give their child the same tenderness, the same nurturing and love, that most mothers do. Being thrust into the new experience stirs to life feelings they never suspected they had.

THE FATHER'S TWO ROLES

The father begins to assume importance now as he becomes real as someone radically different from the mother.

To go back a bit. During the early months, the father had a double role. Around the time when the mother was temporarily subordinating her needs to the baby's, the father subordinated his needs to the mother's and nurtured both mother and baby.

In the beginning, no matter how much a mother while pregnant may have looked forward to the arrival of the baby, it takes time for her to get used to the new demands that were thrust on her, seemingly relentlessly. Some demands, in fact, can never be gotten used to and must be stoically endured for a time: as a prime candidate, the nights of unrestful sleep because of feedings (though if the baby is bottlefed the father can help in this respect too).

"Mothering" and its demands are an example of a not very easily changed inequality. During the initial period of parenting, life seems to make things easier for men than for women. But more and more, men are becoming aware of this imbalance and, out of love and caring for their partners, and because it is becoming socially "acceptable" to be more involved in the infant's routine, try to compensate by taking on some of the mothering and give the mother as much moral support and parenting help as they can.

Now—during the baby's toddlerhood—the father becomes the representative of another kind of "someone" in that vast and intriguing Out There that more and more draws the interest of the child. As the father comes into greater focus, he is seen to be not simply another mothering person:

he is a different sort of person. And all the things that distinguish him are interesting: his different voice, his different way of moving, his different smells, the different sense of power he conveys. The child's identifying with these differences helps, then, in fostering separation from the mother: the father's orbit pulls the child a bit more away from hers, and that comes as a change that feels good both to the child and the mother.

"THE LOVE AFFAIR WITH THE WORLD"

As walking becomes easier, the exhilarated explorer wanders farther and farther from home base, and with a heady sense of accomplishment. It feels like a triumph over earlier limitations.

But of course the wandering is cautious and prudently limited. An invisible tether keeps the mother within safe range of the toddler. Periodically the child checks back to assess the physical distance between them. The toddler wants to check the mother's position to make certain she's comfortably near. But the child does something else too: according to the psychoanalyst Heinz Kohut, "When a child moves away from mother and looks back he is not only reassuring himself, he also wants to see her look of pride in his achievement."

The toddler also studies the mother's face to gauge her mood. Security to a toddler means knowing that the mother's love is dependable. Her love is an island of stability in a world of flux. The toddler wants to be sure there is no change in their relations even though great and unfamiliar changes are taking place in the baby's world—both the inside world and the outside one. As the mother continues reliably to offer closeness, both worlds feel safe.

As mentioned, the need for closeness is not just physical but emotional. When the mother gets angry, to the toddler it feels like abandonment. In the toddler's reasoning, the anger is an "attack." And to be attacked is to be abandoned and left for dead. In fact even if it's the infant who gets angry, it feels as if it's the mother who has gone away and left the child. Because: the child's anger inwardly "destroys" her, makes her momentarily the "bad" mother again, which leaves the child with the sinking feeling of being alone in the world.

While observing her and internalizing her moods and attitudes and values, the child learns her way of doing things. The idea of the self builds as the child identifies with her, but identifies in a selective way: some traits don't feel exactly right and are rejected (her occasional anger at the father, perhaps). Others, more congenial, are adopted (her lighthearted view of living).

The world continues to enlarge. As a byproduct of walking—a side benefit, as it were—the angle of vision rises above the sea level of the crawling stage. Now new sights and intriguing objects come within reconnaissance range and reach: the gigantic throw cushions on the great sweep of sofa, the immense plateau of the coffee table, the colossal flower pot and geranium plant at the window that soars upward into the stratosphere.

With many novel objects touchable and reachable under the toddler's own locomotive power, infantile narcissism reaches its height. Aside from affording the excitement of travel, the ability to walk fills the toddler with elation and the feeling that grandeur and omnipotence are perhaps not an illusion after all. Perhaps life was only joking about that.

Feeling intoxicated with an upsurge in abilities and self-esteem, the child acquires a great mission. The writer Henry David Thoreau, the author of Walden, described himself as a self-appointed inspector of snowstorms and rainstorms. The baby becomes an inquirer into all happenings, affairs, objects and events. The guiding principle seems to be that what reaches awareness must be examined, probed, checked out and, if possible, understood then internalized and filed away. The baby's motto seems to be: "If it exists, it's interesting, and if it's interesting, learn why." The psychoanalyst Phyllis Greenacre calls this period "a love affair with the world." Not counting feedings and diaper changes, nothing in the infant's life feels routine any more: almost the entire world is, once again, fresh and new, and marvelous in its infinite stimulation.

This is especially true of the physical circumstances of the environment. As the great initial inventory of the world begins, wall plugs, floor lamps and wires demand particular scrutiny. Other items requiring audit are kitchen sink cabinets and gargantuan drawers containing pots and pans, those remarkably satisfying objects of research that provide opportunities for noisy mayhem. The baby's view of the world is sunny. Like God surveying creation, the baby sees that everything is good—in fact more than good: the toddler would undoubtedly concur with the physicist Robert Oppenheimer's exclamation, "How vast is the novelty of the world, and how much [it] transcends . . . prior imaginings," a thought that will unconsciously accompany each step of development throughout life.

Sure of the mother's protection, the baby excitedly explores the surrounding terrain with boldness, traveling as far away as the tall kitchen doorway to peer into a vasty stretch of dining room, paling away at its far end into a disquieting terra incognita. A thousand daily excursions—from the remote frontier of the washer-dryer to the not quite so distant, less scary territory of the breakfast nook—end in a return to the shelter of mother, the comforting center of the world. To feel her presence up close, to embrace and touch her, fortifies and reassures.

SPEECH AND THE WORD NO

We recall that the smiling response was an indicator that much emotional development had silently been taking place beneath the surface. The baby was becoming "related."

And then came "stranger reactions." At that stage the infant felt not merely related but related to a specific and valued other—the mother.

Now comes yet another major change, touched on earlier: speech—the supremacy of verbal communication in the enjoyment of human relations.

Speech enables the infant to move to a higher level of functioning by replacing action with words. And just as important, with the acquisition of speech comes the enrichment of thought.

The first communications of life are need-expressing global words in which whole sentences are condensed to simple sounds. Ba," for example, depending on inflection and volume, can mean "Mother," "Hi," "I am lonely," "I am happy to see you," "I am hungry," "I am frightened," "Look at me," "Come here," "I love you," and much more. Communication at this level is in the nature of appeal, not description.

As neural connections continue to grow more intricate and the processes of the cerebral cortex mature, words become less global and ambiguous, become, by the age of eighteen months, specific messages. No longer merely need-gratifying utterances, language becomes communication. This new ability opens the way to using speech to convey infinite gradations of wishes, feelings, thoughts, intentions. It is at this age that many parents begin to feel they're relating finally with a human being.

Before long, the infant encounters a word of peculiar importance, one that is often accompanied, in this culture, by shaking the head horizontally: the word no.

Parents use it frequently, sometimes vehemently. It intrigues the toddler. No is the first abstraction in life: it does not point to any object or refer to something you can taste or hear or feel. It expresses negation and is life's second prohibition. (The first prohibition was weaning—if that has already happened, though it can be put off without harm for another year, or even longer.)

Understanding the idea "no" signifies that intellectual progress has begun to accelerate. With gusto and evident pleasure, the toddler picks up the use of the word. The contrariness it seems to give voice to fits in with the child's needs. The parental "No!" expresses power, and a show of power impresses.

Nothing arouses in the child the desire to emulate the parents so much as repeatedly hearing the word no: the sudden "No!" to putting fingers into lamp sockets, "No!" to stuffing something harmful into the mouth, "No!" to impulsively dashing out into the street, "No!" (it begins to seem) to everything.

No conveys the immensely pleasurable feelings of authority and dominance, and the child willingly identifies with the no-saying parents and adopts the word. The delusion of omnipotence, though perpetually being trimmed, is still relatively strong, and that lends to the "No!" a splendid resonance. To a child there is magic in its strength.

The three "organizers of the psyche," as Spitz called them—the smile, the reaction to strangers and the use of speech (and especially "No!" in support of contrariness)—are genetic in origin. They are constitutional givens—our human inheritance. This is worth emphasizing to make sure it is understood that not just the smiles at three months but all, including contrariness, are a part of normal development.

The no-saying coincides with attempts at "leaving" the mother during the "practicing" period. That makes contrariness even more congenial to the toddler: putting them together at this age makes the child feel early stirrings of independence (but only stirrings).

Contrariness helps build autonomy. It is an assertion of individuality, of self. The defiant toddler is saying: "I have a will of my own and count as somebody. I have convictions, and my personal view of life is just as good as yours."

Quite true. In this regard, parents might think of their toddler not just as the baby they have "brought into the world" but as a new and unique creation of the human race, and with all attendant rights.

Spitz pointed out that it is only when you are capable of saying no that your yes becomes an expression of choice. The proverbial "girl who couldn't say no" was not saying yes but merely yielding. No gives meaning to yes.

Contrariness and Power

But contrariness is important for another reason: the toddler continues identifying with you.

Put yourself in your toddler's shoes and you will see that you may be the "contrary" one and all the toddler is doing is imitating you. In the course of a single day you say to your child "No!" or "Don't!" more frequently than you think and more loudly than you're aware. If the toddler's hand reaches for a wall plug, you could not possibly race across the room in time to stop it, so your sudden "No!" covers distance immediately.

Or if something annoying happens several times running—like dropping mashed potatoes from high chair to floor to test whether gravity is as permanently operative as it is interesting—you might finally get irritated and shout, "No, no, NO! Don't do that!"

The toddler tries to fathom what you're communicating. And the urgency with which you utter the monosyllable visibly impresses the young new sensibility. When you shout "No!" the small, toddling body stops dead, one outstretched hand frozen in midair, as a fascinated gaze is directed back toward you and at the change that has suddenly come over you. Your "no" feels like an aggressive act to the toddler, interrupting pleasure. And, the toddler wants to know, by what right?

The toddler, ever impressed by your size and strength, wants to emulate you and act with what appears to be your incredible might. In the child's reasoning, to behave like you is to be you. And there is the great bonus: by identifying with you and yelling "No!" in exactly the same way you do, the toddler is no longer forced into the passive mode but can take an active role in life. And that always raises self-esteem.

The toddler's contrariness is not seriously intended as a rejection of you. The toddler gives you credit for being able to take things on the chin and not retaliate: you're the adult. Adults can afford to let the child have the last word, appreciating, as they do, its face-saving importance.

POWERLESSNESS AND TANTRUM

The child's pushing you away, physically or verbally, is an attempt at making you feel the toddler's pint-size displeasure at the struggle between autonomy and outside authority. Autonomy is what the toddler wishes to have and what you want to help build. When autonomy and outside authority conflict, the toddler wants you to feel the conflict, and feel it well—wants you to respect what the conflict implies. The toddler thinks that only if you feel what the child feels will you understand. If anything, rather than rejecting your love, the child's contrariness tests it and confirms it.

Around this age (eighteen months to two years) there begin to be tantrums. As the toddler's perception and thought increase, imagination soars, and fantasies outstrip the ability to realize them. Life reveals more of its richness, and the toddler wants it all.

The discrepancy between what is and what might be dramatizes the child's powerlessness. The toddler continues to believe in omnipotence even though it is challenged at every turn.

And the mother's unreasonable-sounding "nos" and "don'ts" don't help: no more cookies, don't soak the teddy bear in the tub, don't go in that room, stop banging the pot with the spoon, no more pulling books off shelves, don't throw food on the floor. But what sets off a tantrum are not those but typically something quite trivial: the string to a toy is so hopelessly tangled that the toy "won't work anymore!"—loud angry tears. In such moments, life does seem a trial.

CONTRARINESS ONLY A PHASE

Most parents sense the developmental importance of contrariness and allow it to happen. They don't try to stop it, or uproot it, as though it were a defect. It's not. They know that contrariness will play itself out, and development will proceed all the more smoothly for its having been allowed expression rather than suppressed.

The toddler's contrariness may sometimes appear to adults as a personal attack on them—it may in fact be an attack on them. (Parents, seen as omnipotent, are "therefore" the cause of frustrations and deserve to be attacked in punishment.) But attuned parents understand it's a stage. The child is pulling away from them a little—and also very carefully not losing them.

The contrariness is a perfect example (as described earlier) of aggression not as hostility but as a developmental force—providing you permit it and imply that it's acceptable. By granting the child the right to be contrary and yell "No!" (it won't go on forever) you help soften the toddler's aggressive energy as it plays itself out. Your permitting it comes across as an expression of love, and as we said earlier, it's love that tames aggressiveness.

It is probably obvious from everything that has been said so far that development is not merely sequential. It is dependent also. First this happens and then the other happens.

Each change emerges from a preceding change. Every step two is shaped by a step one, and all the steps, from birth to death, are determined by the developmental timetable.

The philosopher William James observed that there is in development a "timely age," and if it "goes by in a sort of starvation . . . the individual grows up with gaps in his psychic constitution which future experiences can never fill." That's because every stage poses a developmental task to be accomplished, and each stage, when its time has come, can build only on the materials it finds in place. If what it finds is inadequate, it has no choice but to build on the inadequate. That would retard progress—or render it impossible.

Nature is replete with examples of the importance of satisfying a given set of needs at a given time. Ethologists report that if a butterfly, emerging from its chrysalis, is prevented from unfolding its wings within a critical few minutes, its development is frozen and it can only walk, not fly.

TIMELINESS IN DEVELOPMENT

In other words, where the environment discourages development, deviation from the norm is inevitable. The bypassed development might become available at a subsequent time, but by then it might be too late for its best effect. A makeshift compensating structure will already be in place, and normal development would be rejected.

For example, in an operation performed in 1728 by the English surgeon William Cheselden, the doctor removed cataracts from the eyes of a young man who had been blind from birth—and Cheselden was astonished that his "cured" patient still could not see. On the contrary, overwhelmed by the new optic sensations, the patient instead became agitated and disturbed.

It was not yet understood that seeing is learned and that the man had spent his whole life "seeing" in some other way. What his eyes began registering after the operation was not the world but painful, blurry movements. What he "saw" seemed awful because it made no sense. The lights, colors and shapes bombarding his optic nerves did not correspond to the world he was familiar with by touch. Touch, the compensating structure, had replaced seeing.

He was so confused by the change that he complained that the images were scraping against his eyeballs. He was unable to coordinate his sense perceptions or distinguish shapes. He couldn't judge relative size, tell parts from wholes or perceive space and depth. He had vision but could not see. Sight had come too late to make sense. To him, the acts of groping and feeling, as a compensating structure, had replaced sight and were "sight." What others called sight was to him only a chaos of stimuli. He was exactly in the position of newborns, in whom some of the sensory apparatus is not yet fully functioning because not all neuronal connections have yet been made.

In a similar case, an eighteen-year-old woman, blind from birth and surgically given sight, did not know what to make of the meaningless profusion of colors and shapes. She wasn't even sure that the strange sensations were coming in through her eyes, until she proved it to herself by closing the lids and discovering that this stopped them.

These examples offer insight into the newborn's experience of vision becoming perception. The difference is of course that back then, in infancy, the appropriate time, the changeover happens smoothly. Perhaps nothing demonstrates so dramatically the importance of timeliness in development than the many cases of those born blind who, on being given sight in adulthood, find the "blessing" so bewildering and excruciating that they ask to have their blindness restored.

WISH VERSUS REALITY

Around the age of two the child becomes aware of existing. The idea pops into consciousness one day: "I'm me and I'm alive." ("I imagine myself. Therefore I am.") With advances in perception and the ability to think have come more of an understanding of how things are.

It's not surprising that this period is notorious for inexplicably sad moods that descend on the child, for the occasional whining of even the most uncomplaining toddler, for temper tantrums and explosive blowups. Acknowledging the gap between the child's wishes and the child's increased abilities brings a hated wisdom: the discrepancy between wish and reality is still just as wide as it ever was, and there's no bridging the two, despite developmental changes and experiences. The unyielding obstinacy of reality, so unaccommodating to egocentric strivings, continues to be fought off. But reality, with infuriating equanimity, conflicts with vanity the same as ever and shows not the slightest sign of capitulating. In the end, the toddler accepts its demands, reluctantly.

Reality can't be denied, not sanely. Reality asserts itself as it impersonally and irritatingly contradicts the child's illusion of omnipotence at every turn. Reality is. Omnipotence has to keep proving itself. And it can only fail.

Finally the illusion of omnipotence gives up. Against a mounting evidence, its fate is inevitable: the illusion goes down to defeat. Reality wins both the battles and the war. The child is forced to concede that "I want it" is never a sufficient reason for getting anything and probably the worst possible method: mere wishing is futile.

Limitations, so crushingly real, can't go on being ignored for long. Life casually undermines all attempts at controlling it—another new insight. As insights pile up and understanding grows deeper, knowledge is not felt to be power, not at first: at first knowledge is more like a bitter pill—how sadly lacking in power one is. This necessary and healthy correction of earlier feelings of omnipotence enables the child to build a new world-view, now on the more solid foundation of what's real rather than on self-flattering fantasies of the great "me."

The period is an unusually sensitive one. The child's enjoyment of separateness and growing autonomy is not unalloyed. In symbiotic union there was the mother's powerful strength to lean on, omnipotence à deux. But in autonomy, this new, untried state of being, there is—what?

THE IMPORTANCE OF DEPENDENCY

The toddler at first does not know what support to use to sustain a newly emerging autonomy. A vast unknown lies ahead. The excitement of a growing independence is tempered by the fear of letting go of dependence. And so dependence is held onto a while longer. That is not self-indulgence but a need, and a healthy one: there is no more ideal soil for comfortable, nonthreatening growth than the familiar.

Put simply, the toddler's need is to be separate but not separated. The need is to be a separate being but not separated from the mother—not yet.

There is probably no greater error in childrearing than to confuse independence with physical separation from the parents—being put into a nursery or left for a while with a babysitter. Independence can't be taught that way. It is not something taught at all, in fact. You can't declare it or train a child into it. Misguided attempts to accomplish that only increase dependency needs, which then persist all the more for being denied. True independence is like true psychological separation: it is emotional, not physical. It comes from within.

Unconscious strivings toward independence need time because like all sound development, independence evolves slowly. It evolves out of dependence. It comes about when the need for dependence exhausts itself. Until then, dependency is not an indication that something has gone wrong. It is a necessary condition and a prelude to independence.

Independence is attainable only when (1) there is an inner mother and (2) the child's identity as someone separate from the mother has established itself.

Until both conditions have been met, separation is premature. Half the child would attempt to fill the role of symbiotic partner to the other half. The self would attempt, futilely, to mother the self. It doesn't work. No toddler knows how to raise a toddler or meet a toddler's needs. And besides, self-love and self-concern, though vital to healthy functioning throughout adulthood, are never entirely satisfying after enjoying the love and concern of another. One is a thin, makeshift experience. The other is so rich it feels as though all of life is in it.

The new is always strange and untested, and the child's caution and conservatism help stabilize the inner world while the strange Out There is being assimilated. That underlines the need for renewed closeness at this time. Closeness helps keep things stable. The toddler can actually enjoy the sense of being differentiated from the mother, can enjoy practicing leaving her if she remains emotionally available for "refueling." Love and closeness reassuringly protect the "all's well" feeling.

The ethologist Jane Goodall, describing how she reared her son, writes that he "was not left to scream in his crib. Wherever we went we took him with us so that though his environment was often changing, his relationship with his parents remained stable."

A child developmentalist would say her son's environment was actually quite unchanging: the parents were the child's portable "environment." It's not surprising that, with no break in their stable relations, she reported her son at four to be "extremely alert and lively, mixes well with other children and adults alike, is relatively fearless and is thoughtful of others." And: "Quite contrary to the predictions of many of our friends, he is very independent." You can almost hear those friends warning her that she was "spoiling" the child, "indulging" the child, and warning her she would regret it later, and so on.

But it is obvious what happened. The rapprochement stage was so thoroughly enjoyed that the dependency need played itself out in its own good time. She stuck to her guns against well-intentioned advice and was rewarded.

PSEUDOINDEPENDENCE

True independence means being able to function alone. And: it is not undone by stress. It holds up once and for all.

Pseudoindependence is a pretending to be independent and believing the self-deception. It is a going through the motions of independence. The person is able to function, but only partially or superficially, and with little pleasure. And the functioning can break down under stress.

Pseudoindependence presupposes emotional pain too hard to contend with. The child makes the decision never to altogether depend on anyone or get too close to anyone. If that means giving up love, at least that's better than enduring pain.

The child feels that if pseudoindependence has its own miseries, it is preferable to being at the mercy of someone. The feeling of helpless need is so unbearable it's best to turn away from external sources of satisfaction in order to avoid severe disappointment. The motto is: Don't expect anything from others, and more than that, don't let yourself need others. You will only regret it.

Obviously a person feeling this way is dependent without knowing it. The dependency, being denied, does not get outgrown. In the emotional stalemate of, for example, both needing the mother and fighting off the need, independence from her becomes too complicated to attain.

There is another difficulty and it too gets buried as an unresolved part of the psyche.

The fear of being dependent on the mother can become so great it boomerangs. The more the child starves for the mother's love, the more urgent the need for her love becomes. When a need reaches a certain intensity with no satisfaction available, it feels threatening. The threat is of being "swallowed up" by the relationship, in this case (unconsciously) getting lost in the mother. Differentiating from her was proceeding well, but it is vulnerable still to regressing to the earlier state of at-oneness with her. The separating self, still months away from individuality, feels like it can be lost.

With this state of affairs, feelings of love that would have gone out to others remain "safe" inside the child and are used up in self-love. The self-love arrests the development that love would have taken in its normal evolution.

During the first thirty-six months of the child's life, love goes through two preliminary stages before becoming mature love.

First: The baby loves the "self": in the earliest months, that's the only form of love possible—a pure narcissistic love.

Second: The baby gradually begins to love the other as long as the other satisfies needs. That's popularly called stomach love, or cupboard love.

Third: The toddler, now three, or three and a half, begins to love the other even when the other is not satisfying needs.

Only this last is real love for another person, who begins to be seen not as an object supplying needs but as a person with intrinsic worth.

When this progression is blocked, the toddler feels a strong pull back from loving the other to the earlier position, narcissism. Narcissism, at this point in development, is age-inappropriate. And it is emotionally dissatisfying—as in the following example.

RONNIE: FORCED INDEPENDENCE AND THE FAILURE OF LOVE

Ronnie, a two-year-old boy, was visibly and bubblingly in love with his mother. In his everyday behavior, you could tell by the way he played and did things that his world was sunny and his enjoyment of life complete.

His mother gave birth to a girl and as a deliberate policy turned away from Ronnie. She told everyone she wanted him to learn to face life by himself. That would make him strong and independent, and he would appreciate it later.

Ronnie's world crashed. Everyone who knew him was struck by his transformation from happy child to someone sullen and withdrawn. He hated his new sister, and with venom. As the years went by, the sister could not comprehend what was happening between them but felt so unrelievedly abused by him that she began hating him back. They avoided each other like poison.

Ronnie hardly ever smiled anymore, a sure indicator of something gone very wrong and calling for emergency attention. But no one seemed to notice. His ignored rapprochement love—or as he unconsciously felt it, his spurned love—soured into rage. On those occasions when he did smile, it was not the happy, carefree smile it had once been but (as one observer described it) "was icy."

His parents, denying cause and effect, began telling friends that they "had been given" a "problem child." "He goes around moody all the time," they complained, and they could not understand what the matter was: he had been "such a good baby." Later they sent him to the "best schools and provided him with all that money can buy," but his "personality didn't improve." They drew the usual wrong conclusion: the mother had waited too long to "teach him independence" and he had already gotten spoiled. She should have been cool toward him from the start and now she had only herself to blame.

Many years later, as a good-looking young man about town, his treatment of women was as cruel as his treatment of his sister had been—as cruel as his mother's treatment of him had been. It was simple and classic in cause and effect. He would become acquainted with a woman and she would grow to care for him, and then—always without warning—he would never see her again. If the young woman tried calling to learn what might have gone wrong, he drove her off coldly. He would afterward go through intense remorse over his actions but feel unable to change his behavior. He even spoke of suicide because he couldn't control his feelings.

Several details stand out about Ronnie. First, his need for love during the critical rapprochement period was not met. Second: although a normal, ordinary aggressiveness had been well on its way to being tamed through his mother's love, its progress was undone. It went from usable energy to hate and a wish to destroy.

Third, his love was blocked and could not evolve. Instead of advancing to a more mature form, whatever love he still felt for others remained at the level of gratifying his own needs. He valued people insofar as they provided him with his emotional needs. His love regressed to self-love: only his feelings mattered, not those of others. It was a self-protective, empty stand.

Complicating things further, he remained negatively attached to his mother (through anger and hate) and his psychological birth and emotional independence became unattainable.

THE RAPPROCHEMENT PHASE

The rapprochement love between mother and toddler in the second and third years is now blooming in earnest and is nothing less than an intense love affair. And both would undoubtedly describe it as one of the most pleasurable experiences in life. Perhaps especially the child: it makes all the toddler's hard lessons of development—the recognition of limitations, the shrinking of omnipotence, the being made to wait, the enduring of frustrations—seem not so important. Those "losses" seem almost trifling and can be accepted tranquilly. Reciprocal love compensates for much.

In this new phase the need to be close to Mother is no longer satisfied by knowing merely that she's somewhere about. The toddler needs to interact with her side by side—energetically involve her by the two of them sitting down on the floor together and playing.

The mother's welcoming the child's need for closeness promotes a feeling of safety in moving ahead. Her love and caring and her being available help to reinforce the child's inner strength. Like food, her love is a form of nourishment. And like food, it is required in goodly amounts and at frequent intervals. What has become just as important to the toddler as not losing the mother is not losing her love.

"Love can do all but raise the dead," Emily Dickinson said. Few things can faze a baby who feels loved. The baby's feeling loved (not just the parents' saying "I love you") satisfies the deepest-rooted of all emotional hungers. An enduring love is a quiet euphoria. It fills the toddler with a brimming contentment. It kindles hope, it inspires confidence in the future and it heightens self-esteem. And just as critical as all of these, the child who feels loved loves in return, and enjoys, not fears, the act of loving itself.

It is not dependence but love when a child runs over and sits in the mother's lap. Or asks to be picked up and carried. Or hangs about wherever the mother happens to be. It is love, not regression, when the child brings a toy to the mother and requests that the two of them play with it together, as though she were of the same age and had the same interests.

The toddler of the rapprochement stage asks that the mother read a book together, or tell that story again about the little boy and girl and the nice Mommy and Daddy and the teddy bear who all took a walk in the woods one day and ended up laughing happily, because instead of getting lost they found that the path led them home again.

There is love in all of this—which is the underlying theme of everything that happens during this time. There is trust too, and admiration, both of which are expressions of love. There is also an immense respect for the mother (which will later translate into respect for women, respect for others, respect for nature, respect for self). There is also a growing love and respect for that slowly emerging substitute mother one step removed: life itself.

SEPARATION ANXIETY AND THE FORE TRIBE

The love for the mother rubs off on living, and eliminates separation anxiety, which Margaret Mahler described as the "most prevalent form of psychopathology in the world." Separation anxiety is especially prevalent in our own society. In contrast, anthropologists tell us that there are some tribes in the world where separation anxiety is rare.

In fact, members of the Fore tribe of New Guinea are said not to suffer any separation anxiety—and incidentally (or maybe not incidentally) are strikingly free of depression. From the beginning of their lives, Fore babies have almost continuous body contact with adults, principally their mothers because of their societal conditions. The mother's lap is the center of activity: the babies nurse there, play there, sleep there and touch and explore their mother's body as much as they do their own. Even when mothers cook or work, their babies continue to enjoy uninterrupted physical contact with them. For these babies, nourishment, stimulation, rest and security are never left unsatisfied. As they grow into toddlers, they move away from the mother in exploratory activity but are free to return and touch home base at will. Anthropologists connect these habits of behavior with the infants' self-confidence later on, in adulthood.

For a lesson well worth learning, we might contrast this with Western babies, who are all too often put down to sleep far from their parents, and alone in the dark. And in the morning, after a hurried breakfast, they are dropped off at daycare. After ten to twelve hours a day there, they are then collected by the (understandably) worn out parents for a hurriedly prepared dinner followed by "quality time" and then bed again. This has become a common scenario and one that does nothing to promote feelings of wellbeing in either mother, father or baby. Psychoanalysts have long noted that separation anxiety has become pandemic in our society.

CLOSENESS AND FREEDOM

Around the end of the second and going into the third year, to make doubly sure of the dependability of the mother's love (which, as we have seen, has now consciously acquired value), the toddler "shadows" her. Surreptitious readings of her face reassure that her concern and love continue in their genuineness and steadfastness, which is as love should be.

The shadowing "undoes" some of their separateness. At the same time, paradoxically, it makes separateness more tolerable.

No one believes in togetherness as much as the toddler of the rapprochement stage. As we noted earlier, in a checking-back pattern from time to time, a swift, all-embracing glance from across the room might suffice to maintain the needed emotional closeness to the mother. Or the child, tied to her by an invisible cord, might trail a few inches behind her as she goes from bedroom to bath, back to the bedroom and then on to the kitchen. As she comes to a stop, absorbed in an activity, the child drifts to a halt somewhere in her vicinity, and plays on the floor, casually ready to move on with her. A patter of feet accompany her wherever she goes. It would be an error for parents to get annoyed at this or think of it as a nuisance, or that they have made a mistake in childrearing. This is love at the age of two.

Then comes the complement of shadowing the mother: darting away from her. For a period of time, the toddler delights in the game of dashing a few feet off, luring her into swooping from behind and gathering the helplessly giggling body up in her arms and bestowing hugs and kisses.

As far as the toddler is concerned, the game could be repeated endlessly. There's something ecstatic about it, as the peals of laughter show: once again the mother "undoes" their separateness. Toddler and mother are reunited. But there's a further wrinkle, a variant in the game. Her swooping the small body up is energetically fought off by the toddler's resistant arms that writhe the surprisingly energetic body away from her chest and force her to set the child down again. In such moments her arms are not protectively encircling arms. They are obstacles to freedom, to selfhood.

This one playful game graphically illustrates the child's need for closeness intertwining with the equally powerful need for autonomy. And of course apart from the pleasure of repetition, the game is delightful because mother and child are having fun together, like any two lovers.

The mother-infant tie at this age is becoming increasingly elastic. The elated child, viewing the enlarging world from a new height and savoring the mastery of motor skills that shortly before were not even known to exist, audaciously moves away from the mother but carefully maintains her, as Mahler says, as a "beacon of orientation." She is the familiar landmark that gives the toddler the feeling that the world is safe.

It takes a long time for the emotional need for reciprocal involvement to play itself out. The intuitively attuned mother, by going along with it, gives ample, repeated proof that she cares. She doesn't let the child merely dart away and wander off somewhere and disappear. She understands that the pleasure consists in the child's dashing away and leaving her behind, providing the "freedom" is followed by renewed demonstrations of love by her catching up with the toddler and restoring closeness.

This builds in the child the necessary inner reserve that will lead to independence—which is now no longer far off. Mother will not always be there, but eventually that will not matter, because an inner "Mother" is becoming unlosable.

The rapprochement period is one of the most complex of any in life because the child undergoes many changes all at the same time.

We might pause to see what is being consolidated by the toddler of around twenty-two to twenty-four months. The child is acquiring language as communication, not just self-expression. Thought is richer, making understanding deeper. Small-motor development in hands, arms and legs is becoming more finely tuned. Knowledge of the limits of the self and body image is becoming surer. Differentiation of the self from the other is progressing. With that, psychological separation is coming closer as identity builds. The intransigence of reality is becoming accepted. The mothering experience, internalized as a continuity of love, is being appreciated in a more conscious way. And love itself, that most satisfying of all emotions, is growing stronger and more permanent. Seldom in life does a person experience so many new and enriching psychological advances simultaneously.

PREMATURE TOILET TRAINING

This is the time too when hands explore the body, and the mind reflects on what they touch. New discoveries are made part of the internal map of the self. Curiosity focuses less now on obvious things like the mouth and more on bowel movements and their products, which means things are proceeding normally. To the toddler, a whole new domain opens up.

And to parents too. By this time, if not long before, they have heard and read much about Toilet Training. But now is not the time to teach a child social acceptable behavior. It would be much too soon to make sense.

Some parents are so concerned to do the right thing that they start quite prematurely, at nine months, or twelve months, or fifteen months—in fact, they are not sure when to start. Reports by other (often competing) mothers, relatives, authors and experts are conflicting. Some advocate beginning at the age of fourteen days. (A highly successful dog trainer once claimed to have "house-broken" her children by the age of three months!) And whenever babies are started, one popular book assures parents that, if they do it right, they can toilet-train their baby in a mere twenty-four hours if they follow the author's advice.

Usually, in claims of this sort, it's the parents who get trained. They learn to keep an eye out for the signs of an imminent bowel movement—as when the toddler halts in the middle of play and an unfocused pensive look comes into the eyes. The parents go dashing across the room and scoop the child over to the potty. Sometimes they even make it in time. As parents get adept at the three-meter sprint, and occasionally a bowel movement does take place in or at least near the potty, they say their fourteen-month-old is "nearly trained now." Often this becomes a competition among mothers, to see whose child is "trained" first.

It is a technique that has never achieved renown for its infallibility. And so some of these same parents also adopt the fallback measure of keeping the toddler sitting on the potty for a half-hour or more. If the child finally happens to have a bowel movement, they take that as confirmation that the toddler is now a "trained baby."

Babies nine or twelve months old can be "trained", that has been demonstrated, but they lose the control they appeared to have acquired, and parents, disappointed but undaunted, start over again. They think they're somehow not following instructions correctly or that they started too late.

Their concern focuses far too much on something that will—if allowed—happen as naturally as the baby's taking the first unaided steps, saying the first word, sleeping through the night: not a moment before the baby is ready.

How "Training" Happens

Training is not learning. Learning involves the child's own participation. You engage interest by allowing the child a say in the process, some assertion of the emerging self. And you don't fight the toddler's sense of power but permit it to be enjoyed. By showing that that's acceptable to you, the child's sense of power will become your ally, making learning easier as you go.

Observant parents know that a child is by nature cooperative and eager to learn. Control, true control, is not something you impose: it can only be attained. And before it can be attained, biology and psychology must synchronize: muscles must mature enough to be controllable, and the child must have the wish to use the potty. To try to impose this before the child is ready is to set the child up for failure, or a sense of inadequacy.

When the biological and psychological components are in place, the toddler is eager to do things according to your suggestions. In bowel control, this necessary meshing of wish and ability happens at around thirty months—that's two and a half years of age—no matter how early you start.

Development, which has its own timetable, will not let itself be forced, and those who try are fighting the toddler's pleasures, which is why the child can't connect toilet training to any kind of necessity.

The wish to use the potty comes ultimately out of curiosity about the parents' own behavior in the bathroom. The parents periodically go into the little room and apparently do something there. Whatever it is, they reappear in a few minutes, sometimes adjusting their clothing. Then one day the wish appears: not wanting to feel left out, the toddler wants to do what grownups do in that room.

It can be that simple, but only toward the end of the third year (24 to 36 months) and only if the child has not felt pressured before then and been made resistant.

THE HARM IN STARTING TOO EARLY

If you begin too early, the toddler hasn't the slightest idea of what you're talking about: you are demanding that the child perform in ways not yet possible, and that creates in the toddler feelings of confusion and incompetence.

And those lead to self-doubt and a sense of inadequacy. Once self-doubt or self-dislike takes hold on the psyche, it requires a constant striving for perfection to combat it: "I should be better than I am"—which, of course, is impossible. But children don't know that and think they are somehow deficient. To strive vainly for perfection only deepens the feeling of incompetence and ironically inspires more self-doubt. As an adult, this is the person who does things extremely well yet is never altogether satisfied with his or her achievements.

These feelings of incompetence and self-doubt in turn make the toddler angry at the parents for their unreasonable demands. More than unreasonable, they are demands that interfere with instinctual pleasures: no small matter.

To the toddler there is nothing disgusting in the sight, smell and feel of feces. The activity has enormous interest at this age (which will later shift to working with clay and doing finger painting). It is a new discovery to enjoy the sensations provided by the rectum and anus and the way they pass their products. "Look!" the child in effect thinks. "I created this." It is understandable that toddlers want to hold on to their bowel movements and store them somewhere. The idea of flushing them away sounds not just ridiculous but incomprehensible. Think what you are asking the child to do: recognize the urge, delay the act while searching for a place suitable to you, next relax the bowels and then when the movement is done, flush away the interesting product produced by the baby's own body so that it disappears forever. The child rightly feels that that's too much to ask.

CONTROL, POWER, MASTERY

This period of development is the first time in life that the child experiences power over his or her environment. Power is heady stuff. Control acquires considerable interest.

The toddler quickly discovers that the parents can neither force nor hold back the child's bowel movements. The toddler has the power not to comply with demands and can defeat parents' wishes by simply holding back on movements. Or the toddler can pause in play and "soil" wherever he or she happens to be standing.

("Soil" is in quotes to remind ourselves that it's a parental judgment: to the child of this age a bowel movement is a fascinating and pleasurable event, not a matter of cleanliness or uncleanliness.)

If parents' love is conditional—if they offer love in the form of approval only if the child "produces" on the potty and is "clean"—the child's self-love will learn to be conditional too. That's what the toddler will take inside and make part of the self. We encounter in life many toddlers who as adults believe they must deserve or merit feeling good.

If the message the child picks up is that instinctual pleasures must be renounced to win parental approval, then self-punishment must inevitably follow. Why? Because instinctual pleasures can't be renounced, not any more than hormones can be renounced: they're there, just as glands are there. Body urges don't stop. Glands, cells, endocrine system, physiology—all of it goes on and on, and therefore conflicts too would go on and on.

THE LATER EFFECTS OF TOILET TRAINING

The reason child developmentalists spend so much time discussing toilet training and when and how it is done is that in the psyche events that develop together get linked together. What matters is not diapers or cleanliness but the ideas—thoughts, emotions—that organize themselves around these events. These ideas contribute to shaping the person's character, personality, values and treatment of others. No one would deny the importance of those developments.

An example from the oral period: the baby who was schedule-fed—who repeatedly felt starved for food and affection—develops a certain outlook based on starving, deprivation, distrust of others, and so on. Such a person might become the executive – or underling – who frequently complains about a lack of "feedback from superiors" and gets angry and suspicious about government regulations that interfere with the "free flow of supply and demand" and thinks of resigning from the organization because job satisfaction seems so hopeless. Granted that that's a caricature, it does illustrate the way a system of "oral ideas" can work. The ideas, which date from the earliest period of life, are of dependence, independence—optimism, pessimism —trust, distrust. And not least, hate and love.

ANAL FUNCTIONS AND IDEAS

Similarly, systems of "anal ideas" could be organized around the experiences of bowel movements, parental demands, and approval (love) that's conditional. These might range from cooperating and opposing, to wasting and hoarding, to being clean and soiling. The individual might, for example, become retentive. Or submissive. Or fastidious. These traits may prove detrimental to functioning in adulthood: they are difficult for others to live with.

To take one set of ideas: elimination and retention. They may continue unchanged throughout life. The original impulses may find direct expression, in the person's toilet habits. There are, for example, adults who have the secret toilet ritual of delaying a bowel movement for as long as they can in order to feel a sexual tension in their colon, although they don't think of it as sexual.

Others go to the opposite extreme, on the side of elimination, and fend off any pleasure of retention. They overly preoccupy themselves with the organs of digestion and imagine themselves to be in perpetual need of "cleansing." They take regular enemas—"colonic irrigation"—and feel considerable emotional lift from doing so.

But also possible are indirect expressions of elimination and retention, having unconscious symbolic significance:

elimination perhaps as the tendency to be self-destructively wasteful with money—its opposite, retention, going so far beyond frugality as to be indistinguishable from miserliness.

Some—labeled "anal personalities"—are fanatic about neatness and cleanliness (the person who vacuums a rug and then goes back and vacuums out the vacuum marks). Others stubbornly resist your wishes and make you wait, a trait that has been called "the power of the powerless." Some maintain a control so quietly obstinate that its intention is unmistakable: an attack on you. Attempts at imposing premature control over bowel movements, then, can have long-range effects on character.

Parents who are concerned about "regularity" might not be aware they're being taken in by an advertising myth. Left to its own devices, the body eliminates when it needs to, whether daily, three times a day, or whenever. Measured against hang-ups, or distortions in character formation, so-called regularity and cleanliness at the age of twenty-four months do not seem very important.

And that is the reason for stressing age-appropriateness in toilet training, as well as the atmosphere and manner in which it is taught. Child developmentalists' concern is not some abnormal preoccupation with human intestines. It's a concern that parents not rush psychological development and create emotional difficulties later. Impatient training defeats itself by harming the person. What's a few months more of diapers and smells when you're dealing with a child's long-term emotional wellbeing? (Anyone having difficulty accepting what is being said here might wonder what his or her personal toilet training experiences were like!)

FURTHER SELF-EXPLORATION

Toilet training focuses attention also on what is to the child a new part of the anatomy, where torso and legs meet: the genitals. This is often the case because when the child is actually sitting on the potty, the exposed parts invite inspection.

The sexual drive is a part of every human being from gestation to death. Physiologists, biologists, embryologists and psychologists all agree on the power and duration of the sex drive. Embryologists note that male fetuses get erections, and many a parent has been amused to see their week- or month-old baby boy show the same unmistakable sign of sexual excitation, sometimes immediately before he urinates.

It is easy to appreciate how normal the curiosity and exploration are if you put yourself in your child's place between the ages of two-and-a-half and three years. To adults it's the toilet training age: their concern is with cleanliness. The toddler has no idea of what is socially desirable, and so the idea "toilet training" can't possibly be explained to the child. But touching and feeling the self—these are quite real.

To the toddler the body is still a learning experience, and exploring and fondling it is a part of self-discovery. And the genitals are no ordinary part: this special "me" experience is one that produces considerable pleasure. As adults we may think this level of "knowledge" is banal but that's because we learned it long ago. To a child the discovery of the pleasures of the sexual apparatus is a revelation, of no less joy than the discovery of hands and fingers at age three to four months—indeed much more so.

SEXUAL CURIOSITY—AND SELF-COMFORT TOO

In the earliest phase of development, the mouth was the primary erogenous zone of the body. The baby's first "sexual", or psychosexual, pleasure was the oral one of sucking. This not-to-be-denied instinctual drive, linked to survival, continues of course to assert itself. This is true even among babies who have been fed on demand: thumbsucking is normal until the child is at least six or seven years old.

The baby's pleasure in thumbsucking is of self-comfort in the period where narcissism is normal. Those who think there is something wrong in this self-gratification would have difficulty in explaining why thumbsucking starts in the uterus, as early as the third or fourth month of gestation.

After the oral pleasures come the anal pleasures, which we just touched on, and then not long afterward, the genital pleasures.

When a boy handles his penis and a girl snuggles her hand between her legs, they learn a bit more about separateness from Mother: they can produce pleasure for themselves, and that is a valuable lesson to learn. In case of psychological need, they are less dependent on her.

In that way the cause of autonomy is further served: not all gratification must proceed from outside the self. "I," the toddler feels, "may be separate from my mother, but that doesn't mean I'm helpless or totally dependent. I am capable."

All the experiential learning that we have been talking about—body image, sense of self, curiosity about living, the acquiring of knowledge, building toward independence—all this can be defeated by the sex-is-dirty attitude. Parents used to think that early curiosity about sex was premature and should not be encouraged but stopped. But parents' slapping the toddler's hand as it touches the genitals subtly discourages the impulse to learn. And parents' denying certain body parts through never naming them (avoiding "touching" them even with words)—the clitoris, the penis, testicles, vagina—has the same unfortunate effect.

Little girls often cup a hand between their legs when they urgently need to pee: it helps until they can get to a toilet. Holding the crotch is a sign that they're learning control. This time-honored gesture produces an incidental sexual pleasure, which is perfectly normal. It's an indication of biological advance. It means that the most pleasurable sensations that the body can yield have begun to be concentrated in the clitoris (or the penis). The shift in erotic site, going from mouth to anus to genitals, comes in ultimate support of the supreme biological function of the species: to survive by reproducing itself.

The whole aim of sex education is to foster an attitude of liking the body—of liking human biology. The aim is to develop loving feelings about sex and sexual pleasure. The best way to encourage those benign and healthy attitudes in the adult is to instill them in the child.

THREATENING ABANDONMENT: A NO-NO

Now that walking is a workaday accomplishment, a parent-and-child stroll through the neighborhood offers novel enjoyments and opportunities for learning about the world. An intriguing doorway raises questions about the physical environment, about openings to pass through. Ants and crawling bugs are fascinatingly Lilliputian and so curiously busy. A leaf fluttering along the ground, pushed by a puff of wind, arrests attention: why does the leaf scrape along in that scratchy way and then flip itself over—and does its doing that have a significance that needs to be understood? The toddler, studying the towering fire hydrant, the high-rise majesty of rows of canned goods on grocery shelves, the varieties and colors of indifferent "big people's" faces hurrying down the street and peering down at the child from the sky, the muddy puddles on the pavement and the dandelion growing in the sidewalk crack—the toddler is enthralled by every bit of it.

On strolls, parents, even though they may be in a hurry to get home, are particularly careful not to make another error in misreading the child. The child is not dawdling or dragging behind on purpose or being contrary. The saunterer is like a meandering river, which, Thoreau reminds us, may appear to be aimless in its course but is doing what all rivers do, seeking the shortest path to the sea.

Attuned parents don't think of it as deliberate dawdling. If you are in a hurry to get back home before the plumber arrives to fix the leak in the bathroom, explain in advance (before you go out) that you can't stay out for very long. During the walk, announce that it's time to go home and allow several moments for that to sink in, with perhaps a friendly reminder in the interval. This makes your child an individual, not someone who is autocratically ordered around. It usually works. If worse comes to worst, you could pick the child up in spite of loud protests, providing you don't do that often. Sometimes you really do have to maintain a schedule, a necessity that no child can understand before a certain developmental age has been reached. But if the day's schedule is so critical, a stroller would be easier on parent and child.

Parents who feel they must use emotional blackmail ("Bye-bye, I'm leaving you here") to make the child rush to catch up with them are probably not aware that that strikes terror into the child's heart. Such threats exploit the child's still-real dread of abandonment, and one or two such episodes would undo long and careful preparations inwardly building toward independence, and can reinstate the need to cling to the mother and to the ways of an earlier time, when life was simpler and safer.

To arouse the fear of abandonment is to instill the feeling that the unknown—all in development that still lies ahead—is to be feared. If a mere stroll down a quiet street can lead to danger, there's no telling what might happen in the still unimaginably large world. Though it may be a fact that the novelty of the world may be vast and transcend prior imaginings, it is also true that the toddler is still

> *a stranger and afraid*
> *In a world I never made*

and at all times needs the reassurance of emotional closeness.

Adults too have the same need.

PSYCHOLOGICAL GESTATION APPROACHING FULL-TERM

Love protects, love reassures, love stabilizes, love invigorates. Love becomes trust, and trust and stability smooth the path of development.

Love increases the feeling of continuity, which the dependent toddler uses as a foundation to build on. With their greater vulnerability, toddlers want love to be demonstrated unequivocally, and often. Feeling loved is their protective shield while they're building independence.

The slow and steady development of love facilitates the three-year-long second gestation leading to psychological birth, which nears now. The child is able to weather and sometimes even welcome brief physical separations from the mother. By this stage, the toddler engrossed in play might barely notice the mother's leaving the room: her brief disappearances don't arouse anxiety. This is not the calmness or pretended indifference at her departure that actually is a cover for anger and revenge. Far from it: this is the advanced stage of development that parents have been working toward all along. The child's autonomy, slowly formed and unsapped by anxiety, is coming into its own.

But to take nothing for granted, we should remind ourselves that like much of psychological development, autonomy is a fluid and reversible achievement. For it to attain strength and become consolidated, it will need continuing parental protection. It is well-known how, in moments of extraordinary stress, an instantaneous longing for the solace of maternal reunion appears "from nowhere." Men mortally wounded in combat involuntarily cry out not for their father or some other powerful male figure but their mother, life's first protector and the never-forgotten symbiotic partner. Less spectacular and more common examples are the wounds suffered in the workaday world: a catastrophic loss of income that momentarily sends the victim to the consoling embrace of wife or mate—so similar, in its expression of need, to the painfully scraped knee that propels the crying toddler to the mother, knowing she cares and will offer compassion.

ALONE BUT NOT ABANDONED

The first three stages of psychological birth have been successfully transited: differentiation, practicing and, longer and more complex, rapprochement. The fourth stage leads to psychological birth.

The child's mental representations of the mother are becoming more permanent. Thanks to her good-enough parenting and her dependable availability, mental representations of the mother no longer fade quickly.

The mother exists in a version of herself that the child carries inside. Before now—the age of three—this idea was either not always available or it faded after too long a separation from the mother. Or it was easily lost under stress. Now the inner representations of her as a loving, caring and concerned person remain alive inside the child, who can press them into service as self-care and -love and -concern.

The dependability and consistency of the mother make it possible for the child to send down a deep taproot of feeling loved—deep enough to withstand the thousands of stresses to come along as a normal part of life. The child builds in fact a capacity to love—to maintain love and enjoy a one-on-one relation with another human being. The child learns this from the nurturing received. As the psychiatrist Selma Fraiberg expressed it:

> *We now know that those qualities we call "human"—the capacity of enduring love and the exercise of conscience—are not given in human biology; they are the achievement of the earliest human partnership, that between a child and his parents.*

This is how love achieves permanence and becomes unanxious and strong. In one of his most passionate sonnets Shakespeare observes that real love is characterized by constancy:

> *Love is not love*
>
> *Which alters when it alteration finds,*
>
> *Or bends with the remover to remove:*
>
> *O, no! it is an ever-fixed mark . . .*

The mother out of sight is no longer a mother out of mind, or worse, out of life. What is said here about mothers applies to fathers also, and eventually to others who matter to the toddler. The child enjoys an inner world, more of smiles and enjoyable feelings, which strengthen, than of frowns and angry attitudes, which incapacitate. Even when fury toward mother (or father) runs strong, erupting sometimes in a wish to leave her, she is never truly "lost."

Because of the close contact between the mother and the child, the representations of the mother inside the toddler no longer wilt even with prolonged absences. She has been well internalized. Representations have had time enough to acquire great durability. That's why her actual physical presence is not so critical anymore: she has become transportable, permanently available because amply internalized. By the preschool age of three or three and a half (even more so at four), she is never absent. The first day of school will pose no great threat.

The mother's transportability gives the child a feeling of emotional support even when alone. Now, and not before now, the child can actually feel solitary without feeling abandoned, can be alone without feeling lonely.

The mother, as someone with a life of her own, can make the statement that "Mommy is tired" and know that that has become a comprehensible idea. The greatly experienced toddler of thirty-six or forty months, having a sense of self, understands the experience "tiredness" and can appreciate what is being said: when Mommy is tired it means Mommy needs a rest. This vicariously experiencing the feelings of others is another notable achievement. The toddler has acquired a capacity for empathy.

Empathy is perhaps the most valuable of all human qualities. Empathy underlies parents' wish to nurture their child and explains why, as Winnicott points out, that out of billions of births, so few of the world's children suffer severe emotional disorder.

Approaching Psychological Birth

Early childhood is nearing completion. Starting now the child will strongly resemble adults emotionally—a mark of great progress. The infant who came into the world psychologically "incomplete" has become capable of empathy—an immense advance. With empathy, the maturing toddler begins to recognize the self in others and others in the self—a development of enormous sophistication.

And the child begins now to take over parents' behavior and attitudes as these engage the interest of the young and curious in-gathering mind. Adopting their mannerisms and style of expression, the "senior toddler" becomes the specific child of specific parents. And if parents are loving and considerate, so will the child be.

Empathy reveals its origins in love: it links the child's own enjoyment of life with the other's enjoyment. Love is real only when consideration of the other goes so far that one's own satisfaction is impossible without the other's. There are faint glimmerings now of the child's moral feelings—empathic caring—toward the mother, and toward a growing number of others.

The maturing toddler, having established an identity, has a feeling of belongingness and at-homeness in the now more clearly perceived huge world beyond the mother—out there but rapidly growing inside the child. The child lives in ever more clearly distinguishable versions of the two worlds, the inner and the outer, and with comfortable familiarity loves and enjoys both.

THE BIRTH OF THE INDIVIDUAL

Psychological gestation reaches full term, if all has gone well, some time around the beginning of the fourth year—after the thirty-six months of differentiation and practicing and rapprochement have been successfully passed through and consolidated. By this time, feeding, sleeping, bowel movements, a certain amount of body hygiene and the avoidance of bodily injury have all become the growing child's own concern—incidentally lightening the load of parental care.

Development has come far. In retrospect, the importance of meeting the infant's emotional needs during the early months can be appreciated. That experience underlies the perception that relations between humans are satisfying. People fulfill themselves through each other. And what satisfies and fulfills works toward the ultimate pleasure of harmony in human closeness.

The child doesn't just abstractly know this: that would be cold and inadequate, not true knowing. The child has become capable of feelingly understanding this. The knowledge, however unconscious, is that human relatedness is a give-and-take of love. Love is the tender yet powerful force that "holds" and protects and nourishes, and makes emotional life a quietly exciting experience. And it powers still further development.

With these great inner changes in place, the second gestation has reached full term. The child unanxiously, and even boldly and adventurously, starts life now as an autonomous human being. Psychological birth has taken place.

Babyloving

Notes

Source material is cited by means of selected catch phrases in the order of their occurrence. One or two short quotations in the text meant as illustration are not cited below for verification, and in these few instances, text references are omitted.

"*Children . . . are not adults*": Joseph Goldstein, Anna Freud, Albert J. Solnit, *Beyond the Best Interests of the Child.* New York: Free Press, 1973, p. 13.

"good-enough" parents: the phrase coined by Donald W. Winnicott, the British pediatrician-psychoanalyst.

"*the consciousness of something there*" and "*the bare interjection*": William James, *The Principles of Psychology.* Cambridge, Mass.: Harvard University Press, 1983, p. 657.

"*[e]ach time the baby*": Louise J. Kaplan, *Oneness and Separateness: From Infant to Individual.* New York: Simon & Schuster, 1978, pp. 90-1.

"*touchingly expressed in the infant's*": Phyllis Greenacre, "Considerations Regarding the Parent-Infant Relationship," in *Emotional Growth*, Vol. 1. New York: International Universities Press, 1960, p. 208.

"*No, the baby is dead*": *Time,* March 19, 1973.

"*transitional object*": D. W. Winnicott, "Transitional Objects and Transitional Phenomena," *International Journal of Psycho-Analysis, 34* (1953), 89-97.

"*The 'Custom's Inspector'*": S. Brody and S. Axelrad, "Anxiety, Socialization, and Ego-Formation in Infancy," *International Journal of Psycho-Analysis, 47* (1967), 218-29.

Coney Island Hospital: San Francisco *Chronicle*, Feb. 20, 1980, p. 2.

"*The first of my wants*": *Confessions*, Part Two, Book 9.

Acquiring certain abilities: see Jean Piaget, *The Psychology of the Child*. New York: Basic Books, 1969.

"The motion picture made": Selma Fraiberg, *Every Child's Birthright: In Defense of Mothering*. New York: Basic Books, 1977.

Holy Roman Emperor Frederick II: This material derives from Ashley Montagu, *Touching*. New York: Harper & Row, 1972, p. 98.

stable human bonds: Some have experimented with babies just to see what language babies might "naturally" speak if they don't hear adults' baby talk and cooings. (The word *naturally* gives pause.) According to Herodotus, one such experiment was conducted by Psamtik, a seventh-century B.C. pharaoh, who isolated two infants in a mountain hut in the care of a servant instructed on pain of death never to utter a word to them. As it happened, the very first syllable either of the infants spoke sounded to the servant like the Phrygian word for *bread*, from which Psamtik, who liked his science unambiguous, concluded that if parents don't teach their babies the language they themselves speak, babies spontaneously talk Phrygian.

Another experiment was made by King James IV of Scotland, in the sixteenth century. He hoped to prove how venerable Scottish tradition was, and was delighted to discover that the babies of Scotland spoke Hebrew before they moved on to Celtic, which meant that Scotland's heritage was ancient and therefore its people—don't look for logic—should support the royal establishment.

"*As late as the second decade*": Ashley Montagu, *Touching*. New York: Harper & Row, Perennial Library, 1972, pp. 93-4.

"*The absence of accustomed mother*": James L. Halliday, *Psychosocial Medicine: A Study of the Sick Society*. New York: W. W. Norton, 1948, pp. 244-45.

"*Dr. J. Brennemann*": Montagu, *op. cit.*, p. 95.

The material on differentiation, practicing, rapprochement and object constancy is based on *The Psychological Birth of the Human Infant*, Margaret S. Mahler, Fred Pine and Anni Bergman, New York, Basic Books, 1975, passim.

"*The Love Affair with the World*": Phyllis Greenacre, "The Childhood of the Artist: Libinidal Phase Development and Giftedness," in *The Psychoanalytic Study of the Child*, Vol. 12. New York: International Universities Press, 1957, 27-72.

"*When a child moves away*": Heinz Kohut, oral communication: tape made shortly before his death.

The passage on the word *no* derives from Spitz, *op. cit.* and *No and Yes*, New York, International Universities Press, 1957.

"*the timely age goes by*": William James, *The Principles of Psychology*, Cambridge, Mass., Harvard University Press, 1983, esp. pp. 1017-1022.

The passages on blindness and restored sight are described in Spitz, *The First Year of Life, op. cit.*, 277-85. The passage on Spitz's work with marasmic babies derives from "Hospitalism: An Inquiry into the Genesis of Psychiatric Conditions in Early Childhood," *The Psychoanalytic Study of the Child, 1*, 1945, and "Hospitalism: A Follow-Up Report," *The Psychoanalytic Study of the Child, 2* (1946).

"*was not left to scream*" and "*extremely alert and lively*": Jane Van Lawick-Goodall, *In the Shadow of Man*. Boston: Houghton Mifflin, 1971.

The material on how love evolves from narcissism to need gratification to object constancy derives from the work of Heinz Hartmann.

"*a stranger and afraid*": A. E. Housman.

"*We now know that those qualities*": Selma Fraiberg, *op. cit.*

AND IN GENERAL:

The phrase "psychological birth" is from Margaret S. Mahler, Fred Pine and Anni Bergman, *The Psychological Birth of the Human Infant*, New York: Basic Books, 1975, passim. Also from that work are: "hatching," "shadowing," "checking," "darting away," "senior toddler" and "beacon of orientation." "Refueling" was coined by Margaret Mahler's colleague Manuel Furer.

"Holding experience" is from D. W. Winnicott, *Holding and Interpretation*, London: The Hogarth Press, 1986, passim. Also in *Home Is Where We Start From*, New York: W. W. Norton, 1986, esp. pp. 107 and 145-9. The latter work is also the source, *inter alia*, of the "good enough parent."

"Trust and strangeness": Otto Fenichel, *The Psychoanalytic Theory of Neurosis*, New York: W. W. Norton, 1945, p. 88.

The passage about Halloween masks derives from René A. Spitz, *The First Year of Life*, New York: International Universities Press, 1965, p. 86. All discussions on "eighth-month anxiety," "stranger anxiety" and "organizers of the psyche" are based on Spitz, *ibid.*, Ch. VIII, and Spitz, *A Genetic Field Theory of Ego Formation*, New York: International Universities Press, 1959, passim.

The phrase "aggression of developmental force" is Phyllis Greenacre's.

Bibliography

Ariès, Philippe. *Centuries of Childhood*. New York: Vintage Paperback, 1962.

Bowlby, John. "Maternal Care and Mental Health, "*World Health Organization Monograph Series No. 2*, Geneva: Palais des Nations, 1952.

——. *Attachment*. New York: Basic Books, 1969.

——. *Separation*. New York: Basic Books, 1973.

——. *Loss*. New York: Basic Books, 1982.

Brody, Sylvia. *Patterns of Mothering: Maternal Influence During Infancy*. New York: International Universities Press, 1956.

Brody, S., and S. Axelrad. "Anxiety, Socialization, and Ego-Formation in Infancy," *International Journal of Psycho-Analysis*, Vol. 47, pp. 218-229.

Brazelton, T. Berry. *Infants and Mothers: Differences in Development*. New York: Dell Publishing Company, 1973.

Buchwald, Art. "Reminiscences," in Jacqueline Bernard, *The Children You Gave Us*. New York: Jewish Child Care Association of New York, 1973.

de Mause, Lloyd, ed. *The History of Childhood*. New York: The Psychohistory Press, 1974.

Dillard, Annie. "To Fashion a Text," *in Inventing the Truth*, William Zinsser, ed. Boston: Houghton Mifflin, 1987, pp. 53-76.

Eiger, Marvin S., and Sally Wendkos Olds. *The Complete Book of Breastfeeding*. New York: Bantam Books, 1973.

Elkind, David. *The Hurried Child: Growing Up Too Fast*. Reading, Mass.: Addison-Wesley, 1981.

Erikson, Erik H. *Childhood and Society*, 2d ed. New York: W. W. Norton, 1963.

——. *Identity and the Life Cycle*. New York: International Universities Press, 1959. In *Psychological Issues I*, 1959.

Fraiberg, Selma. *The Magic Years*. New York: Charles Scribner's Sons, 1959.

——. *Every Child's Birthright: In Defense of Mothering*. New York: Basic Books, 1977.

Freud, Anna. *Normality and Pathology in Childhood. In The Writings of Anna Freud*, Vol. VI. New York: International Universities Press, 1965.

——. "Psychoanalytic Knowledge Applied to the Rearing of Children," in *The Writings of Anna Freud*, Vol. V. New York: International Universities Press, 1969. Ch. 16, pp. 265-80.

——. *The Psychoanalytic Treatment of Children*. New York: Schocken Books, 1964.

——. *Research at the Hampstead Child-Therapy Clinic and Other Papers, 1956-1965.* New York: International Universities Press, 1969.

Freud, Anna, and Dorothy T. Burlingham. *Infants Without Families.* New York: International Universities Press, 1944.

——. *War and Children.* New York: International Universities Press, 1944.

Freud, Sigmund. *The Complete Psychological Works: Standard Edition.* London: Hogarth Press.

Gerard, Alice. *Please Breast-Feed Your Baby.* New York: New American Library, 1971.

Greenacre, Phyllis. "The Childhood of the Artist: Libidinal Phase Development and Giftedness," *in The Psychoanalytic Study of the Child*, Vol. 12, 1957, pp. 27-72.

——." Considerations Regarding the Parent-Infant Relationship," in *Emotional Growth*, Vol. 1. New York: International Universities Press, 1960, pp. 199-224.

Goldstein, Joseph, Anna Freud and Albert J. Solnit. *Beyond the Best Interests of the Child.* New York: Free Press, 1973.

——. *In the Best Interests of the Child.* New York: Free Press, 1975.

———. *Beyond the Best Interests of the Child.* New York: Free Press, 1977.

———. *Before the Best Interests of the Child.* New York: Free Press, 1979.

Greven, Philip. *Spare the Child.* New York: Alfred A. Knopf, 1991.

Hartmann, Heinz. *Ego Psychology and the Problem of Adaptation.* New York: International Universities Press, 1958.

Jacobson, Edith. "The Self and the Object World: Vicissitudes of Their Cathexes and Their Influence on Ideational and Affective Development," *in The Psychoanalytic Study of the Child*, Vol. 9, 1954, pp. 75-127.

———. *The Self and the Object World.* New York: International Universities Press, 1964.

Kaplan, Louise J. *Oneness and Separateness: From Infant to Individual.* New York: Simon & Schuster, 1978.

Klaus, Marshall H., and John H. Kennell, *Maternal-Infant
 Bonding.* St. Louis: C. V. Mosby, 1976.

La Leche League. *The Womanly Art of Breastfeeding.* Franklin Park, Ill.: La Leche League International, 1963.

Leach, Penelope. *Your Baby and Child.* New York: Alfred A. Knopf, 1984.

Liedloff, Jean. *The Continuum Concept.* Reading, Mass., Addison-Wesley Publishing Company, 1977.

Macfarlane, Aidan. *The Psychology of Childbirth.* Cambridge, Mass.: Harvard University Press, 1977.

Mahler, Margaret S. *On Human Symbiosis and the Vicissitudes of Individuation.* New York: International Universities Press, 1968, p. 18.

——. *Memoirs.* New York: Free Press, 1988.

Mahler, Margaret S., Fred Pine and Anni Bergman. *The Psychological Birth of the Human Infant.* New York: Basic Books, 1975.

Medawar, P. B., and J. S. Medawar. *The Life Science.* New York: Harper & Row, 1977.

Miller, Alice. *For Your Own Good: Hidden Cruelty in Child Rearing and the Roots of Violence.* New York: Farrar, Straus & Giroux, 1984.

Montagu, Ashley. *Touching: The Human Significance of the Skin.* New York: Columbia University Press, 1971.

——. *Life Before Birth.* New York: Signet, 1973.

Piaget, Jean. *The Psychology of Intelligence.* London: Routledge & Kegan Paul, 1950.

———. *The Construction of Reality in the Child*. New York: Basic Books, 1954.

———. *The Psychology of the Child*. New York: Basic Books, 1969.

———. *Behavior and Evolution*. New York: Pantheon, 1978.

Princeton Center of Infancy and Early Childhood. *The First Twelve Months of Life*. Frank Caplan, General Editor. New York: Grosset and Dunlap, 1973.

———. *The Second Twelve Months of Life*. New York: Grosset and Dunlap, 1977.

———. *The Parenting Advisor*. New York: Anchor Books, 1978.

Provence, Sally, and R. C. Lipton. *Infants in Institutions*. New York: International Universities Press, 1962.

Provence, Sally, and S. Ritvo, "Effects of Deprivation on Institutionalized Infants,' in *The Psychoanalytic Study of the Child*, Vol. 16, 1961, pp. 189-205.

Ribble, Margaret A. *The Personality of the Young Child*. New York: Columbia University Press, 1955.

———. *The Rights of Infants: Early Psychological Needs and Their Satisfaction*. New York: Columbia University Press, 1943.

Rousseau, Jean-Jacques. *Émile*. London: Dent, 1911.

——. *Confessions*. New York: Modern Library, 1943.

Schaffer, Rudolph. *Mothering*. Cambridge, Mass.: University Press, 1977.

Simpson, Eileen. *Orphans: Real and Imaginary*. New York: Weidenfeld & Nicolson, 1987.

Spitz, René A. "Diacritic and Cœnesthetic Organization: The Psychiatric Significance of a Functional Division of the Nervous System into a Sensory and Emotive Part," *Psychoanalytic Review*, 32, 1945, pp. 146-162.

——. "Hospitalism: An Inquiry into the Genesis of Psychiatric Conditions in Early Childhood," *in The Psychoanalytic Study of the Child*, Vol. 1, 1945, pp. 53-74.

——. "Anaclitic Depression: An Inquiry into the Genesis of Psychiatric Conditions in Early Childhood in Early Childhood II," in *The Psychoanalytic Study of the Child*, Vol. 2, 1946, pp. 313-342.

——. "The Smiling Response: A Contribution to the Ontogenesis of Social Relations" (with the assistance of K. M. Wolff, Ph.D.), *Genetic Psychology Monograph*, 34, pp. 57-125.

——. "Relevancy of Direct Infant Observations," *in The Psychoanalytic Study of the Child*, Vol. 10, 1950, pp. 215-240.

———. "The Primal Cavity: A Contribution to the Genesis of Perception and Its Role for Psychoanalytic Theory," *in The Psychoanalytic Study of the Child*, Vol. 10, 1955, pp. 215-240.

———. *A Genetic Field Theory of Ego Formation*. New York: International Universities Press, 1959.

———. *The First Year of Life*. New York: International Universities Press, 1965.

———. *No and Yes*. New York: International Universities Press, 1957.

Spock, Benjamin. *Dr. Spock Talks with Mothers*. New York: Fawcett World Library, 1961.

———. *Baby and Child Care*. New York: Pocket Books, 1988.

Winnicott, Donald W. "Transitional Objects and Transitional Phenomena: A Study of the First Not-Me Possession," *International Journal of Psycho-Analysis*, 34, 1953, pp. 89-97.

———. *Mother and Child*. New York: Basic Books, 1957.

———. *The Maturational Processes and the Facilitating Environment*. New York: International Universities Press, 1965.

———. *Playing and Reality*. New York: Tavistock, 1982.

——. *Home Is Where We Start From.* New York: W. W. Norton, 1986.

——. *Holding and Interpretation.* London: The Hogarth Press, 1986.

Van Lawick-Goodall, Jane. "The Behavior of Free-living Chimpanzees in the Gombe Stream Reserve," *in Animal Behavior Monographs*, Vol. 1, p. 3.

Zetzel, Elizabeth R. "Depression and the Incapacity To Bear It," in *Drives, Affects, Behavior*, Vol. 2, ed. Max Schur. New York: International Universities Press, pp. 243-274.

About the Author

HIAG AKMAKJIAN is the author of *30,000 Mornings* (novel), *Snow Falling from a Bamboo Leaf* (on the art of haiku), and short stories. He was for many years the author of the newspaper column "Babyloving" in a Q&A format as a help to parents on infant and child development appearing weekly in the "Monterey Herald" (California).

His book on childrearing, *The Natural Way To Raise a Healthy Child*, was a selection of three major book clubs: Book of the Month Club, Psychiatry and Social Sciences Book Club, and Psychology Today Book Club.

The Princeton Center for Infancy and Early Childhood places his name on the dedication page of its much-praised parenting book *The Second Twelve Months of Life* alongside the names of Anna Freud, Benjamin Spock, Selma Fraiberg, and T. Berry Brazelton.

www.ingramcontent.com/pod-product-compliance
Lightning Source LLC
Chambersburg PA
CBHW060519030426
42337CB00015B/1945